ARE YOU MISSING PEACE?

GIRISH JOSHI

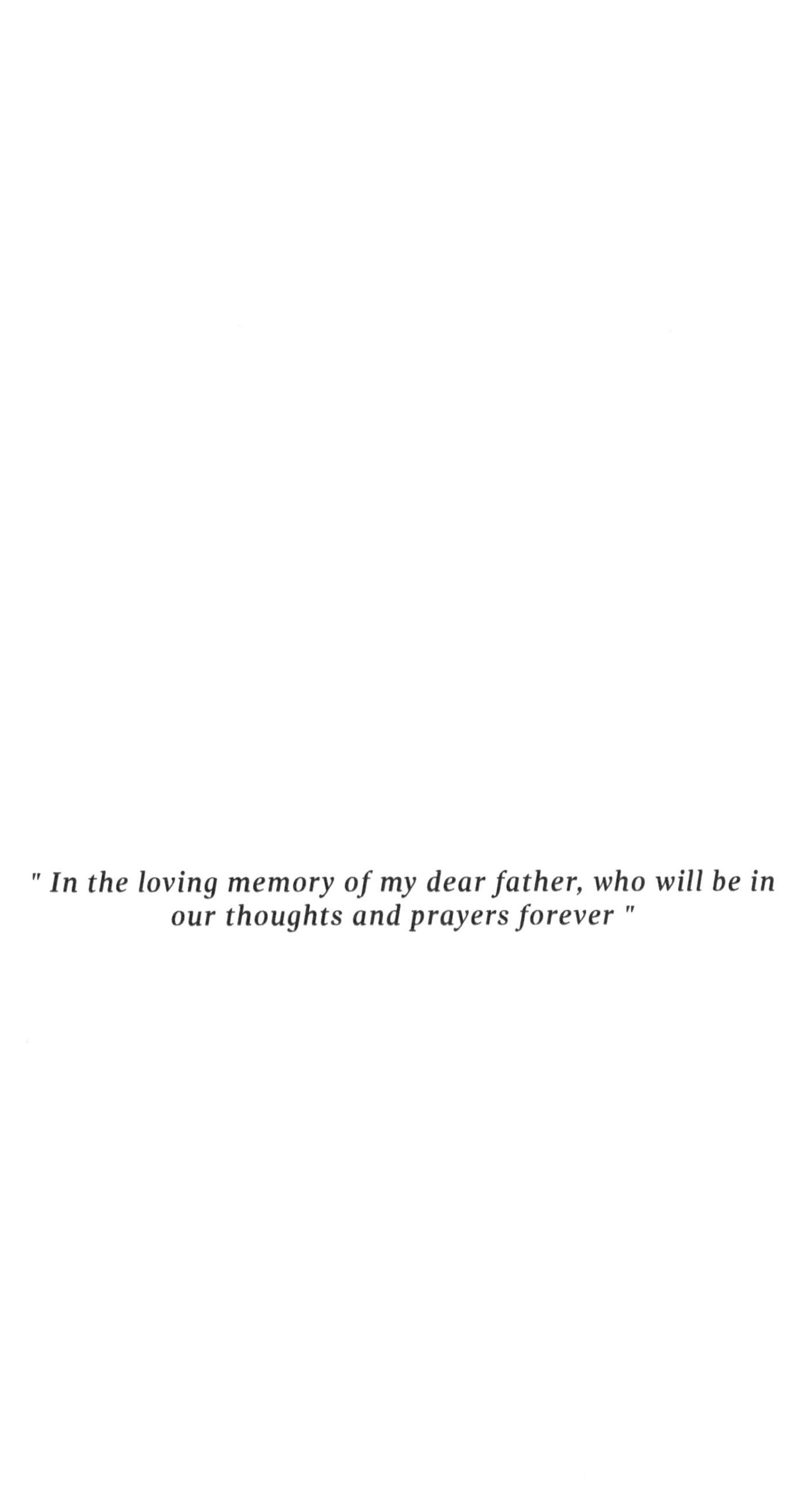

" In the loving memory of my dear father, who will be in our thoughts and prayers forever "

Contents

Foreword — *vii*

Preface — *ix*

Acknowledgements — *xiii*

1. The Context – Quick Recap Of Bhagavad Gita — 1

2. Fear, Doubts And Confusions In Life — 5

3. Learning The Basics Of Life — 12

4. Importance Of Karma Or Duties — 20

5. The Power Of Intelligence — 25

6. Choosing The Right Karma — 30

7. Managing Disappointments: Understanding Our Mind — 35

8. The Illusion Of Maya — 42

9. Understanding Death, Next Life And Liberation — 47

10. The Divine Knowledge: Connecting The Dots — 52

11. Decoding The Power Of Almighty — 57

12. Experiencing The Divine Form Of God — 61

13. Understanding Devotion: Find Qualities That God Loves — 66

14. Understanding Our Body And Soul — 70

15. How Our Behavior Changes With The Qualities Of Prakriti — 81

16. Understanding Our Spiritual Dilemma — 87

17. Human Behavior: Good And Bad Side Of It — 92

18. Identify Right Faith, Food, Sacrifice, Austerity And Charity — 96

19. The Ultimate Gyan And Conclusion — 101

20. Understanding Our Belief System — 108

21. Hundred Golden Questions & Their Answers For Inner Peace — 111

About The Author — 155

Foreword

WHO SHOULD READ THIS BOOK?

This book is for everyone who is facing challenges in life and finds it difficult to cope with stress. This is for people who are missing inner peace and are disturbed in their life.

Everyone must read this book if any one or more of the following conditions applies to you: -

- If you are facing continuous challenges in life and are upset with it
- If you are missing inner peace
- If you have questions about life, death, spirituality, afterlife
- If you have not read the Bhagavad Gita even once but have some spiritual interest
- If you have read the Bhagavad Gita but have not understood it fully or left it in middle
- If you doubt spirituality
- If you have a logical or cognitive mind that is unable to relate life with God
- If you are under stress, depressed or confused
- If you have faced depression symptoms or undergoing anxiety-related treatment
- If you are unsure where is your life is heading to
- If you hesitate to ask others or are afraid of seeking help
- If you are too frustrated with life or lack trust in others

Preface

WHY I WROTE THIS BOOK?

I have been successful personally and professionally in my life. Life has always been very kind to me. Right from setting new academic records to various professional accomplishments, I have achieved almost everything which I desired in life.

I was always under the impression that I can handle any tough situations, take bold decisions, and manage conflicts and interpersonal relationships. My five decades of life experiences had been enriching and they enforced my beliefs based on various situations that I had faced and managed in my life successfully. However, life took a new turn about four years back when one incident broke me to the core. I was terrified, became depressed, and, hopeless with life. This was related to a painful and unimaginable demise of an individual with whom I was deeply attached since my childhood and the one who shaped my upbringing. I am talking about my father here. The intent of this book is not to talk about the details or specifics of the incident but rather to share the learnings which one can use in similar situations in life when you feel helpless, hopeless, and not able to decide what is right or wrong for you.

I was in a state of loneliness and shock (you may call it depression) for almost one year post this incident. When you have been asked to take a decision related to the continuation or termination of life for an individual whom you love the most, nothing can get as bold or bigger a decision as anything else. You either take the guilt of either killing someone with your decision or prolonging the sufferings of your dear ones indefinitely under tough medical conditions. We decided to end the artificial life for my father. My dad struggled for his death for over seven days without ventilator support, without food, without water, without artificial oxygen in immense pain at home. This was beyond the medical explanation. Medically, doctors have indicated the probability of his death within 2-10 hours post artificial support removal but there was something else written for him by God. He struggled for seven days for his death. I had witnessed him dying very closely for seven consecutive days, every moment, every minute; sitting next to him; sleeping next to him. It was a very painful, devastating experience. We even prayed to God multiple times to take him away as we could not tolerate the pain and his struggle in front of us.

During that phase, I had so many questions about life, its struggle, pain in life, death, and beyond but I could not get those answers anywhere. People around me tried to convince me but that bothered me more than before. No one was able to convince me of the bitterness and uncertainties of life, and why such things happened in my life all of a sudden, I had no convincing answers anywhere and I finally tuned to Bhagavad Gita to find my answers. And yes, I did get all my answers after three years of continuous struggle, search, and immense pain post that incident. I am sharing my learnings here. It was real hard learning. This book is not a spiritual Gyan nor the regular stories of Gita or explanation of its verses that are available freely on the internet or in many mythological books on Gita. It is rather a guide for everyone to handle tough situations, take bold decisions, and understand the real meaning of life, its shocks, and surprises. It gives clarity to thinking by applying the principles of the Gita to any situation.

We all are busy chasing our dreams and goals. In the ongoing quest of becoming successful, rich and powerful, we often forgot about the real things that we need the most from life that would give us ultimate peace and satisfaction. The sad part is that we have constantly changed or moved our goal post in the competitive world and we are still not satisfied. We need more and more in life. The richest men on earth are still chasing more wealth, people like you and me are chasing ways to live a better life or secure our future. However, we all have not defined "what is enough for us?" The other sad reality is that we are not prepared to face the shocks and surprises of life. We are not prepared for our death. We defer this subject. Our quest is not to understand life but rather find more and more accumulations in life for satisfaction. We chase it in form of a top position in the job, or a successful business, enough bank balance or settled kids, or a perfect retirement. And the result still is in form of our continuous dissatisfaction, fear, anger, jealousy, greed, emptiness, stress and depression in life in some form. We may not admit it openly but that is the reality.

We all are vulnerable. We think we are strong but in reality, we are not. We have perfected living a fake life that is so impulse-driven that we are not able to manage the uncertainties and shocks of life at a personal level. We pretend we are happy and strong but many of us are not. Many times, we do not know what to do, how to deal with tough and painful situations or decide what is right or wrong for us. Bhagavad Gita learnings can help here. All we need is to understand it, relate to it, and use its guidance.

Let's navigate the learnings together and find your answers here related to any challenges in life that you have doubts about and beyond using Bhagavad Gita principles! It took me over 15 months to put this book in current shape after reading multiple variants of Gita books and other Vedic literature repeatedly. Trust me, you will get most of your answers related to life in this book for every doubt or question on yourself, your life, sufferings, luck, death, and beyond.

The Bhagavad Gita is the divine treasure, the supreme knowledge that has been told by the Supreme Almighty, Lord Krishna to his devotee Arjuna and compiled in the Indian Vedic repository about 5000 years ago. However, due to its complicated verses, Sanskrit language, and length, many of us find it difficult to read, interpret and digest. Many of us start the mythological or spiritual book but leave it in between. It took me over 3 years to decode Bhagavad Gita and I still find new knowledge and learnings evetime I read it. This book is written with the intent to explain and help the principles of the Bhagavad Gita that can be applied in real life. Even if this book can help a single person in his life, I will consider writing it a worthwhile effort of mine.

I am thankful for indirect and virtual learnings from Swami Mukundananda (founder JKYog) and Swami Prabhupada (founder ISKCON) and various other Vedic books and videos on topics of Bhagavad Gita. This book is an attempt to decode and demystify the Bhagavad Gita for everyone who believes in God or wants to understand life or wants to find the answer to a question in life that relates to them but is struggling with getting a satisfactory answer. This is in plain English with a simple explanation that you can relate to your personal and professional life, without emphasis on the verses or the dialogues of the Bhagavad Gita. The aim is to make us immune spiritually in this physical world to face any kind of situation. And to attempt to purify our current life with a meaningful purpose, gratitude to God, and selfless care for others.

Acknowledgements

This book is dedicated to my father "Mr. Damodar Joshi" who has been my inspiration during my entire life. He is the reason for this book.

My sincere thanks to Swami Mukundananda (founder JKYog) and Late Swami Prabhupada (founder ISKCON) who have been spreading the knowledge of spirituality across the globe. Their learnings, various books on Bhagavad Gita and spirituality, videos, and lectures have inspired and guided me to understand Gita with clarity and put this book.

Last, but not least, this book is dedicated to my family who has always inspired me to stay positive in life. Special mention of my wife "Geetanjali Joshi" who stood by my side during difficult times giving her unconditional support and love.

CHAPTER I

The Context – Quick Recap of Bhagavad Gita

Bhagavad It is practiced, followed, and learned across the globe, across various religions making it a unique global reference of learning and living life meaningfully. The broader high-level understanding and interpretation of people for Bhagavad Gita is that: we all are going to die someday, so we must live a superior life that is without any worry, guilt, shocks, and surprises of life. As per Hindu mythology, our soul will travel to heaven and we get punished or rewarded for our deeds. So, we must do good acts in our current life. Every religious text promotes such learnings to do good actions or karma and be kind to others, so what is so unique here? The answer lies in the context.

If things are so simple, why we do not follow or practice them and ignore it? Many of us are not able to relate to the actual narratives of Bhagavad Gita. The 700 verses in Bhagavad Gita which was written in the Sanskrit language are very deep in meaning but complex and give an explanation of various situations that comes in our life and how best to deal with them. The Bhagavad Gita is a set of dialogues and knowledge also called the song of God. It is the guidance offered by a teacher (Lord Krishna who was an incarnation of Lord Vishnu) to his student Arjuna who was filled with moral dilemma and despair about the violence and the death in the battlefield during his fight with his kin. While Bhagavad Gita does not promote violence, it guides you to fight against injustice in the society for the betterment of everyone. We must do the right Karma without fear of the outcome as results are anyways not in our control.

Gita is not about generic gyan rather it gives you practical steps and tips to deal with any situations in life. No matter the kind of situation you are in or dealing with, you will find your answers and solutions to your problems, concerns, pain, stress, depression and any miseries in life will have an answer in Gita. All you need is to follow a few simple guidance and recommendations from the Gita which are not too difficult to relate and practice. One may not attain divine supremacy and purity in current life but an attempt that can give immense peace and mental satisfaction in any situation is worth exploring.

Let's recap the quick background. Arjuna was not able to decide whether to fight or quit or give up in the war when he was fighting against people that included his dear granduncle, teachers, and kins. It was a power tussle to gain the control of the kingdom illegally, forcefully captured by his kins (Kauravas). When all avenues of diplomacy and peace failed, war became inevitable between two groups. Different groups were forced to support their respective kings or leaders due to a variety of reasons and personal agendas.

Our life is also driven by similar circumstances and we make different decisions and make choices (good or bad) based on our interpretation of right and wrong or based on our greed, desires, selfishness, anger, and revenge. The way we think is often reflected in our behavior. Many of such aspects are driven by our belief systems and surroundings. Our belief system continuously undergoes changes and it either improves or degrades based on situations and circumstances that we face and our actions in those situations. Irrespective of our choices or decisions that we make, if we are not at peace within ourselves, there is no value in anything in our life. Gita helps us differentiate clearly on what is right for us and how best to make decisions. It makes us prepare and face any situation without worrying about the outcome.

There are numerous narratives and interpretations of the Gita but the ultimate message has not changed over centuries. It revolves around how to decide what is right and wrong for you, what are our real duties, how to purify ourselves (our karma), how to be just and impartial, how to handle any tough situation and how to make ourselves mentally strong for any situation in life.

It guides us to pick meaningful and right Dharma (Righteous Duties), refrain from Artha (materialist or economical gain mostly money related) and contain our Kama (desires or lust that gives pleasure) to attain Moksha (Liberation). The way we think and act governs our life.

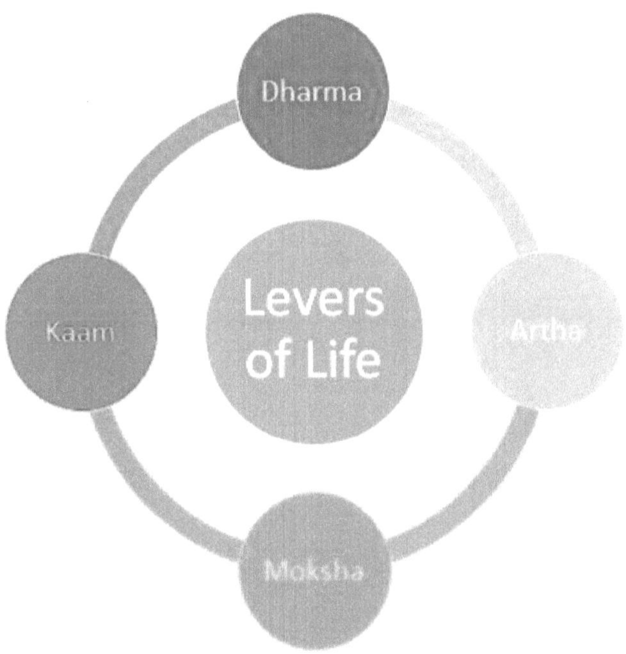

Levers of Life

The right and wrong are mostly our perspectives and viewpoints on individuals, groups, and religion. The good news is that we can change our perspective and thoughts over time. Gita does not force you to pick specific actions rather it gives you choices and helps you differentiate and identify the right choice for you and also warns you of repercussions. It helps you make yourself mentally strong in any situation.

Each chapter of this book is an easy-to-relate situational map for you and helps guide how to handle it using Bhagavad Gita principles and narratives. We all find it difficult to read actual Gita books due to their deep and complicated meanings, Sanskrit language, verses, complexities, meaning, and varied interpretation. However, we can relate it easily to a various similar situation in our life and how best to navigate as per principles from Gita.

This book and an attempt to achieve that. This is based on my three years quest and struggle to find the "why of life" which I faced personally and how best to handle situations, shocks, and surprises after reading various mythological and spiritual books including readings of variants of the Gita.

The learnings included have helped me and I hope you will find it a useful tool to make your life meaningful and enriching.

CHAPTER II

Fear, Doubts and Confusions in Life

We often overestimate our capabilities and are under the illusion that we can handle or face any tough situation. Arjuna was the most capable, mentally stable, and powerful warrior who at the same time was very kind at heart as well. He had full control over his "Sleep patterns" (he was called Gudakesh, the one who had conquered sleep patterns) with his mental strength indicating he was mentally very strong. However, when the time came to fight his kin, teachers, elders and family members (Kaurava) for ethical and moral reasons, he lost his control and mental abilities. He became confused, emotional, fearful, in-doubt, and went into a state of confusion, guilt, and depression. (This is Vishad situation indicating the state of sadness, confusion, fear and self-doubt). Arjuna was not sure what is to be done in such a situation? What is going to be right for him and what is not? What should be done and what should not?

As an individual, we often face similar situations in our life. The decision that we take during such circumstances, defines our character, our strengths and values. Confusion is not weakness but rather a reality in life. If someone says, he or she never gets confused, the person is lying to himself. Arjuna was a warrior and he had entered the battlefield to fight a war against the enemy for a just cause. But, upon seeing his family members and dear ones on the enemy side, his rational mind became conflicted and his emotional mind overpowered his decision-making abilities. His attachment and emotions intensified towards his teachers, relatives, great grandfather and family members. And as a result, he struggled with his decision-making. He got confused between performing right and wrong duties. He got so worried about imagining the future outcome, destruction and death from the war that he almost felt he will be at fault if he participates in the war. He preferred to give up his life during the crucial time of the war instead of fighting the enemies. Our attachment to various relations in our life (kids, parents, spouse, friends, relatives) whom we love and care, often becomes reasons that hinder us from performing the right duties. Emotional dilemma is common in our life.

We are driven by our emotions or feelings. Greed, anger, power, lust, sadness, attachment, jealousy, etc are different emotions that we have developed over the years since our birth. Not all emotions are negative or bad. Kindness, care, happiness, trust, empathy, etc are good emotions. The emotional mix makes us confused, many times, in fact, all the time. And most of the times our decisions are based on WIFM (What's in it for me) or how can I get some benefit or is it going to harm me or my dear ones in any way? Many times, fear of failure or negative outcomes forces us to take or support biased, partial, or incorrect decisions. And we often go around to defend ourselves and our decisions. "I am right and you are wrong" kind of thinking or ego is so ingrained within each of us that we do not like the positive feedback, we think of personal gain all the time and we are not ready to listen to others. In short, we are very selfish and self-driven.

In a tough situation, similar to that of Arjuna, when we are emotionally heavy, we either prefer to run away from the situation or give up so easily. In other cases, we defer the decision-making or avoid the confrontation and fail to do our duties timely. Arjuna preferred to surrender or give up even before the war rather than fighting the enemies for a just cause. Does the situation sound similar? Have you also experienced a similar situation in your life?

Our brain is a complicated structure. The decisions are based on hundreds of signals that influences our decision-making. There are 5 key lobes or regions that process various signals in each brain (hemisphere) which we call as Left and Right brain. In reality, there are thousands of pre-processing that happen on each signal which moves between various lobes within the brain. It includes Frontal, Parietal, Temporal, Occipital, Brain Stem and Cerebellum. The final decisions are governed by the Frontal lobe which works as the executive (CEO of the brain). So, decision-making is an extremely complex process.

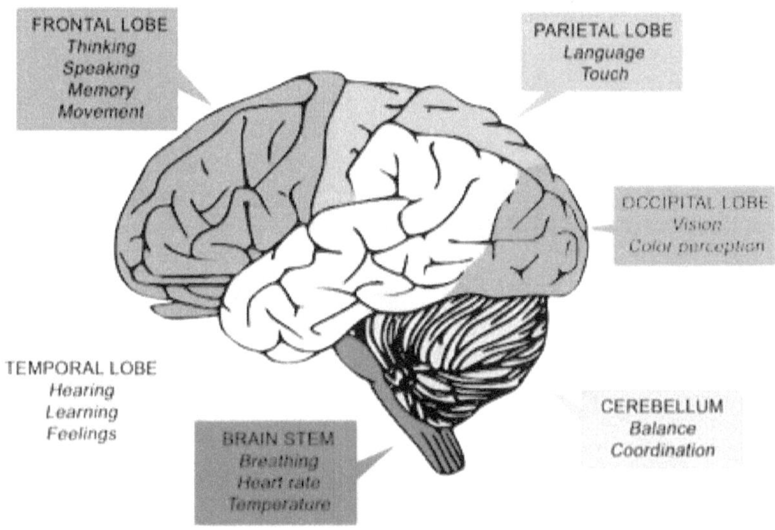

Understanding the basics of decision making of Brain

We often call the left and right brain making distinctive decisions for humans. But in reality, the decisions are made by the whole brain as one unit. The emotions or feelings are handled by the mid portion of the brain (temporal lobe and the areas below it) and those signals are sent to the frontal lobe to think and assess further and make a final decision. If we have more influence of emotions in our life, our brain is more likely to make emotional judgments. Rational decisions are also based on how holistically we perceive the situations based on our experience and what kind of rational signals (strong or weak signals) are passed to the decision-making process of the brain. The past memory, experience, feelings, our state of mind and environment all work together to make a decision. So, if you struggle with decision-making, it is ok. It is a very complex thing.

Many of us have that problem, very few people would admit it openly. We should try to understand our brain a little bit. The idea here is not to appear for a medical exam but rather to understand our brains and emotions and their processing to some level so that we can learn something about our problems with handling emotions.

Emotions are triggered by Amygdala (the portion inside the temporal lobe area). This is a physical structure within our brain. Refer to the picture here is which is in green color. The Amygdala helps us to assess the threats around us.

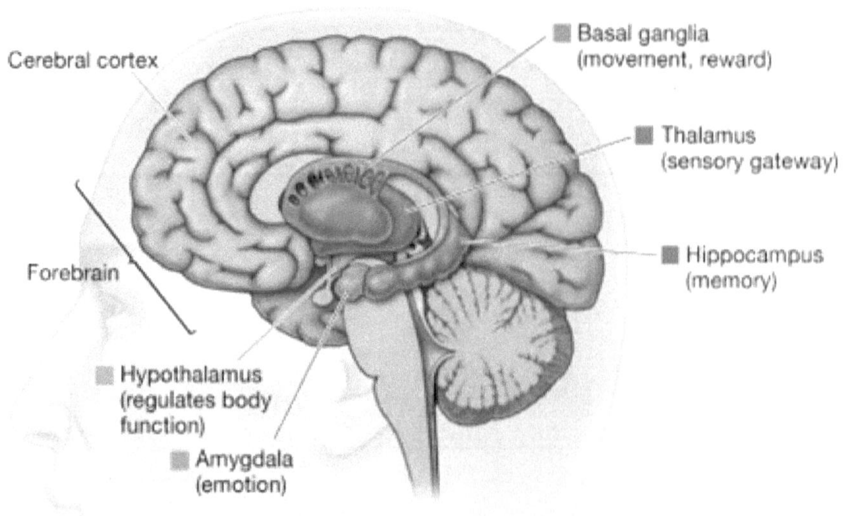

How emotions affects our decison making

The sensory signals (what we hear, see, touch and smell from the environment and people around us) often activate the amygdala within our brain to assess the danger level of a situation. These emotional signals often result in one of the actions i.e., **fight, flight (run away) and freeze.**

Amygdala interacts with frontal lobes (which are executives of the brain) and influences it to make a final decision after sending danger (SOS/ distress signal) to the frontal lobes) and the executive (frontal lobe) The frontal lobe assesses the memory data (facts checking of presence of similar distress) and when it finds records/patterns of such aspects, it gets influenced and instructs the amygdala to fight back the situation and assures support of every part of the body.

Amygdala sends the distress signal to the hypothalamus which triggers the stress hormones secretion in our body (via a gland called the Pituitary gland attached below the hypothalamus). These hormone spreads in our entire body in nanoseconds. And our body reacts to these hormones in form of our actions such as a panic attack, severe stress, feeling lonely or isolated or rejected, feeling like running away or harming someone, depression or at times committing suicide.

People often forget that brain is being designed not just for regular decision-making but also to warn us against the "danger" situation which could be life-threatening. Fight, Flight and Freeze are natural reactions to handling such dangers for survival. We have made ourselves so vulnerable to emotions that we treat or perceive most negative situations or reactions as life-threatening acts. The brain treats and processes every negative emotion similarly and the natural body reaction is the secretion of stress hormones that results in our fear, anxiety, depression and other aspects. And our body reacts to it accordingly.

This is our poor state of handling negative emotions. The bad experiences (past bad emotional experiences) are stored in our memory (Hippocampus) as short-term as well as long-term memory along with other portions of the brain as well. We must be careful in terms of what we want to feed to our brain and stop ourselves from storing negativity into our memory etc or repetitions. Such aspects become patterns and long-term memory over time and influence our thinking and behavior completely. We must remind ourselves that any odd situations (bad feelings) need not always be a life-threatening and reinforce these learnings into our brain/memory and must learn the practice to ignore situations at times.

Most of the time, our feelings are not life-threatening. We must remind ourselves of this repeatedly. This is the best way to get hijacked by emotions. This is the best way to get control over negative emotions. Reinforce ourselves with thoughts such as "this is not life-threatening", "This can be ignored", "I can handle it", etc. Such thoughts can flush out the old memory (negative experiences) over time and we can learn to handle emotions in much better ways. This improves our decision-making. We should not do not perceive everything as a danger to us or our lives and avoid getting trapped by amygdala hijack (Amygdala hijack happens when our brain reacts to psychological stress as if it's physical danger)

The state of doubt, fear and confusion are continuously haunting us in our life similar to that of Arjuna. The fear of negative emotions or imagining a negative outcome makes us weak. And many times, due to such emotions, we fail to take the right decisions for ourselves. And we get into stress, depression, sadness and self-doubt mode. The good news is this is normal for every human being. You need a method to deal with such aspects. And Gita teaches us such methods systematically which are covered in subsequent chapters with clarity.

Here is a learning and quick reference for this chapter: -

- Fear, doubts and confusions are normal to the human being. Even the most powerful individuals are not immune to it
- We must control our negative emotions as it always provides us wrong direction or path. Never take any crucial decisions under the influence of emotions
- We all have limitations and shortcomings. We must seek help from others whom we respect trust, and find intelligence. One should find a teacher or mentor in life. (Arjuna took the help of Krishna as a mentor and teacher to guide him)
- Our confusions are our dilemma to pick between right and wrong. When we think and assess situations as WIFM (what's in it for me) motto by keeping our interest at the forefront, we are almost wrong in performing our duties honesty. The outcomes are never in our control but we can control our greed and biased behavior
- We must stick to our duties that are principle or Dharma based (i.e., righteous). While the perception of right and wrong would change from person to person, the principles are universal. Principals would remain true to every situation. They are universally accepted truth and ethics. Righteousness is the core foundation of Dharma.
- We must own our decisions and its outcome. Never blame others for your decisions and their impact on us or our family. We always have choices in life. We just need a barometer to assess if our decisions are emotion-driven or intelligence based.
- We should never give up easily. Running away from the situation or quitting is not the solution. Such aspects are bound to hit us badly in some other form.
- It is always better to face the situation with the right mindset, accept the reality and do our duties without getting too emotional or worried about the outcome. We have no control over any outcome in our life but we can control our emotions for sure.
- Life is a situational map, and it will never go as per your wish. Be ready and prepared for surprises, shocks and uncertainty in life and face it with

courage and a logical mind.

- A sound decision is made when we utilize our entire brain capacity with little influence of emotions in our judgments. Everything is not life-threatening always; we must remind ourselves.
- Negative emotions can be identified if we are aware of ourselves, their harm to us and understand why such emotions are triggering. Any kind of negative situation can be handled in life.
- The brain is always playing tricks with us. But it is our brain and we are master of it, so we need to learn to get it under our control. Moment, we lose control of our brain (due to negative emotions) and we are bound to make wrong judgments. And such things harm us.
- The best thing is to avoid making judgments when under influence of emotions. Things can wait, life is too precious. Fear, doubts and confusions are normal in life.
- When too many thoughts or negative emotions choke our brain, the best thing is to distract ourselves and get engaged with stuff we like such listening to music, sleeping, exercising, swimming, taking a walk or meditating etc. Take medical help if needed.
- At the end, we must remind ourselves that it is just the hormones that are impacting us which can be controlled. It can be cured naturally as well as medically. Nothing is wrong with anyone. We are a perfect creation of the god.
- Negative thoughts are not bad things as it gets generated without our knowledge, it is our mind that trick us that we fail to recognize or realize. It is the thoughts, the hormones and the mind that are confusing us. It is those negative emotions which is the culprit. We must neutralize it somehow. We are not slaves to our emotions.
- We can control our emotions. Let's not produce negative hormones in our body repeatedly that harm us. Life is beautiful, learn from it, understand it, improve it and enjoy it.
- Life is too short to get worried rather spend it for a more meaningful purpose. Not everything is life-threatening all the time, so our assessment of our poor state is largely wrong
- Let's understand life and its meaning in the next chapter

CHAPTER III

Learning the Basics of Life

Life is a journey. A journey between birth and death. Every human being has to taste the bitterness, happiness, loneliness and shocks of life. There is no exception here. Our life continuously changes. Nothing is permanent in life. Happiness and sadness are like seasons that come and go. Those who understand it are more prepared to face life and can absorb shocks in life with ease. When we are over-attached to individuals and materialistic things, our conscience does not allow us to think beyond ourselves or our relatives. However, that is the key reason for every pain and grief that we face in our life. The more we desire, the more we get inclined toward accumulations, self-interest and greed. And there is no end to it.

We do not want to lose anything in life. Be it our accumulation, wealth and people whom we love deeply. However, we forget to realize that nothing is permanent and death is inevitable. While we get it to some extent but we take it too casually. When the whole society around us is chasing materialistic things, we do not want to be left behind. It has become fashionable today to accumulate for the future so that when the time comes, we have some backup. The majority of humans today are living under such beliefs. There is another category of people that promotes the "You only live once" philosophy. Such people want to enjoy life on their terms without too much thinking or critics from others. In short, both these categories are running behind desires to fulfill their dreams and none of them are wrong. But are they really happy, free from pain, grief and mentally strong? The answer is no.

We are born for a purpose. Yes, this may sound a bit overwhelming. Do we know our real purpose in life? Ask yourself with honesty and we will have no answers here. We may have a fake answer for the world. What many of us call purpose is not the real purpose but rather what we need from life and the extreme end goal of our wish list. However, as per Bhagavad Gita, the purpose of our life is to purify ourselves. Our life journey is an ongoing cycle of birth, death and rebirth. Each of us has a Karmic account that we are carrying for various timeframe and our current life is an opportunity to settle the debt of past karmic accounts. It is an opportunity given by God to purify ourselves so that we attain liberation (Moksha or

Mukti). In short, you get "freed up" from the painful cycle that we face between birth, death and rebirth. The purpose of life is the purification of self to attain salvation i.e., freedom from the cycle of birth and rebirth.

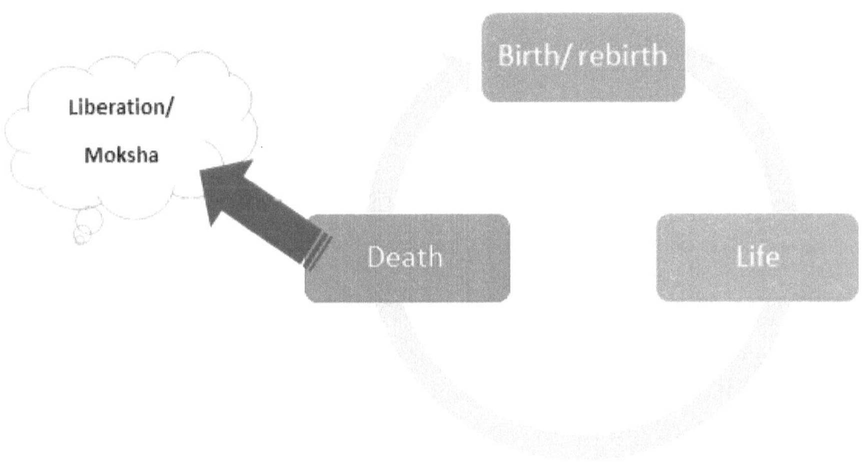

Cycle of birth, Reirth and Liberation

If you do not believe in the concept of Karmic account or fate or karmic bondage or past debts of karma, then ask yourself why someone is happier and wealthier than you, why few are born with physical disabilities, and why some people always face an ongoing struggle in life despite hard work and sincerity, why few are born with golden spoon, why few have a terrible married life or childhood, why some fetus die within the womb of the mother before starting a life journey, why few experience sudden accidents and death in the family? These all questions are related to our karmic debts and karmic account.

The more positive our past Karmic account, the better our current life. It is proven in Vedic scriptures that we take continuous births even after death. There are 8.4 million species in the world and one may take births and rebirth in form as any of those species post-death. The only distinction here is the form or shape of these species which we commonly refer to as the body. The body is born in different shapes or forms. You may call it a body of a lion or a cow or a butterfly or even a human body. Humans are the most advanced form of species and we have gained this advanced form after going through the 8.4 million birth and rebirth cycles. While this is stated in

Veda's thousands of years ago, our science and technology are able to count the species in this early as close to 8+ Million.

Our modern science is still not able to relate to the birth and rebirth cycle and will never reach there as it verifies everything as evidence. And rebirth is not yet proven by science and technology. And when belief systems of the spiritual world and existing facts/evidence of scientific mismatch, one cannot reach reconciliation or consensus. Where the logic reaches a dead end, devotion starts. Everything cannot be proven by science yet. And things that are not yet proven, do not mean it is wrong or non-existent.

Just that it needs more and more time to prove things does not make them irrelevant. Medical science is studying the human brain for the last 7-8 decades and still has not reached even 10% of knowledge around how it is formed or works end to end, how it gets developed automatically during birth in such a comprehensive, complex way, who has created it? There are many unanswered questions in this world, so when the logic end, we must start believing that someone has created things, someday, systematically. This unknown power is God. There is some superpower, somewhere. Not everything has happened just because of the big bang. There are mysteries and one of the mysteries, we call God, the Almighty, the supreme power!

Bhagavad Gita is based on the foundation of soul, birth and rebirth which our medical science does not believe in. It does not mean that something that is not proven yet is wrong, it is just that our knowledge, intelligence and research have not reached the highest level to prove such aspects. In the future, new innovations and experiments might prove such aspects of the spiritual world, soul, etc. Everything is driven based on the belief system. Medical science is still not able to answer how and from where a fetus gets a heartbeat or life after 6 weeks of gestation within the mother's womb. Medical science still does not prove where the life energy disappears or goes after the death of a human being.

But Bhagavad Gita has such answers readily available thousands of years ago for every mystery in this world. We are not formed just because of the planetary explosion or out of a black hole concept. If you look inside your body, the interconnectivity of body organs, the blood supply, the coordination of lungs, heart, brain, cells, womb and recreation of new life within a mother, it has not happened out of explosion or merely coincidence. Every human has similar machinery, similar body parts, anatomy and functioning. This is being designed with perfection by God.

We are special.

Bhagavad Gita makes a clear distinction between the immortal nature of the soul (which is eternal and imperishable) and the physical body. Our body gets survival energy from the soul. When the soul leaves the body, the human dies. Death is inevitable. Death only destroys the physical body of a species but the soul continues its journey. Just as a person discards his old clothes and adorns new ones, the soul keeps changing bodies from one lifetime to another. Soul receives its energy from the almighty whom we also call Paramatma. It is like the sun that provides rays of light and every corner of the world to brighten it. But the sun and rays are different. The Paramatma is universally present everywhere both outside our body as well as within us in the form of an aatma or a soul. The soul is a portion or part of God and is as very pure as God. Our actions performed by our bodies makes it's surrounding contaminated.

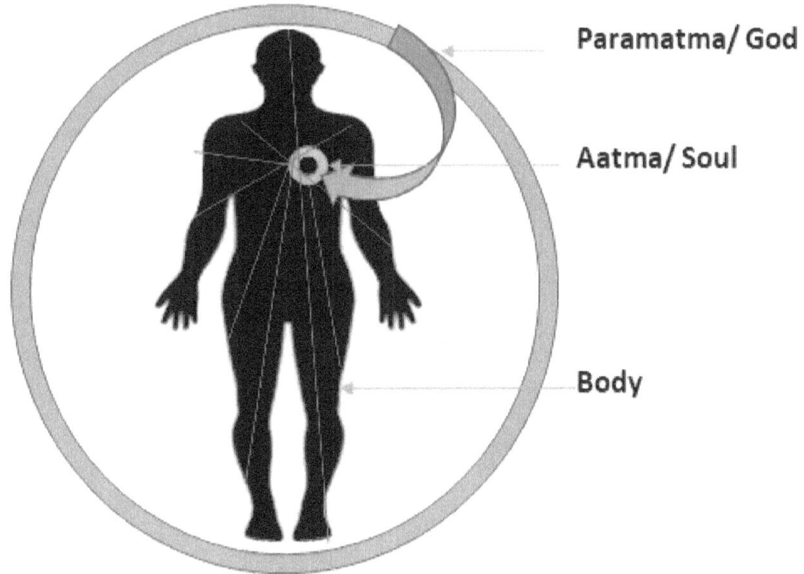

Soul providing energy to entire body

The broader answer to why you face pain and grief in life, is primarily due to our poor karmic account and past karmic bondages which still carries the old debt which you need to settle in your current life. It is up to us to either make attempts to purify ourselves and enrich our karmic account or ignore it. No matter what is our belief system, it is true that when we face difficulties in life, we need a reference guide or a teacher who can help us navigate the challenges. Gita provides such guidance. It helps us how to make ourselves immune to the shocks, fear, stress and depression of life. All we need is some trust and make some efforts to begin the journey.

Happiness and distress are inevitable in human life and are caused due to our past karmic bondages. But good news is these are not permanent and one must learn to tolerate them without being disturbed. One can definitely make attempts and perform good karma to purify them and clear the debt of karmic bondage of past lives. The person who is able to manage happiness and sorrow with ease without getting impacted is eligible for liberation. If we are able to maintain a mental balance, we can face any difficult situation. We must continue our duties without getting impacted by the outcome. The outcomes are not in our control but efforts are something we can definitely manage. We must do our duties with honesty and integrity under any circumstances. In case, we are cheating on our efforts, someone is definitely watching us which is our own soul that resides within our body.

The soul is the portion of the almighty (aka Paramatma) that empowers our body and gives us the energy to live and survive. When the soul leaves a human structure, we become just a dead body. Death is inevitable so are the pain, happiness, aging and disease in life. One must accept this truth. Either we die early or our relatives leave us too early. God has set the timings for everyone, so when there is a call or recalls, the soul departs the body. There is no way one can stop it. Instead of getting into depression due to sudden loss, one must absorb the shocks and convince ourselves that the poor state of our life is either due to our poor luck, past karmic bondages, or expecting too much from life is only invitation to more pain. We are not always at fault in our current life, just that few are punished for the deeds of their past lives or past karma. You must have witnessed sudden death or accidents of a child, newborn or young relative in your entire life. Sometimes there is no answer to why such things happened to them? And if we take it on a logical note and make attempts to make convince ourselves to stay resilient to situations, we can overcome bad lucks either in this life itself or in future lives. All you need is trust, faith and belief in God. God has always been kind to everyone. We have been given this life because we expected it or there were some pending desires that we aspired for in our past life.

The only way to improve ourselves is to perform our duties without any attachment and without any expectation of the outcome or returns and without any fear. This is not easy in today's world where we often think of personal gain as the first thing for any action. This needs a different mindset. The only way to convince yourself is by realizing and acknowledging that you do not control any outcome. In spite of all your hard and sincere efforts also, you might not get what you expect. The pain is not due to the hard effort but rather due to the absence of the returns that you expected for your efforts. The problem is not with the efforts but rather with the desires that are attached to every action that we perform today. We must learn to limit and finally contain our desires for a happy and peaceful life. We must discard all selfish desires and cravings of our senses for pleasure and try to make ourselves free from attachment, fear and anger. This is the real wisdom for happiness and inner peace. All we need is control of our mind and our senses.

Arjuna was in the dilemma of what are his real duties. His attachment to his elders and teachers was the reason that was preventing him to perform his duties. He forgot to realize that as a warrior his duty is to fight the enemy and the unjust without worrying about the outcome of the war. Krishna gave him consciousness and knowledge about the immortal nature of the soul, the cycle of birth and rebirth, the inevitable form of death and the courage to face the difficult situation by clearly going by duties without any distraction, attachment, fear and worries about the outcome.

In our lives also, we face similar situations where we are unclear about the real meaning of life, the reasons for our sufferings, the reasons for not getting rewards or adequate return for our efforts and people cheating around us. This is normal. All we need is to control ourselves, our senses and our desires without worrying about the outcome to live a peaceful life. With a balanced mind, we can control ourselves. The "trap of destruction" is depicted in the picture that every human being face in current life. If we are clear on how to navigate it, we can win the war that we often fight with ourselves.

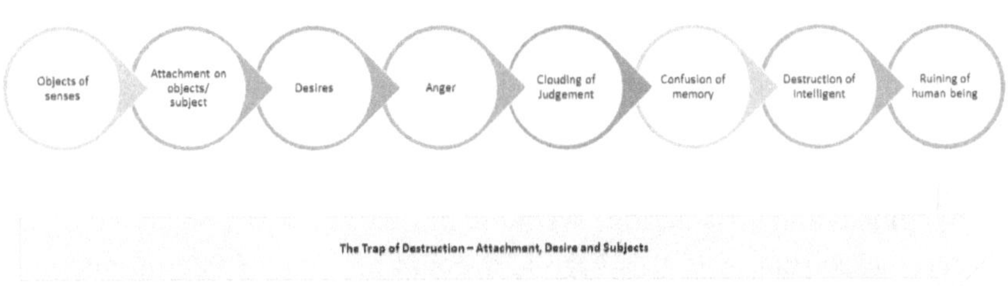

The Trap of Destruction – Attachment, Desire and Subjects

Trap of Dectruction of Life

We need control over our senses so that the attractiveness of subjects does not derail us. With this, we limit our attachment to various subjects and contain our desires. Our mind can help us realize the trap of destruction and with our logical mind, we can control ourselves and the impact of attachment and desires on us. All we need is the practice to control our senses.

Desires are like fire, if they get fulfilled, they get amplified and if they get contained, they are harmless. The one who understands this equation is prepared to live a peaceful life and attain inner peace in every situation. In case we fail to contain our desires, our anger erupts. The anger clouds our judgments causing confusion in the memory. When someone is angry, he is bound to make mistakes or hurt someone. Anger ultimately results in the destruction of our intelligence. With poor intellect, we make wrong choices that are harmful to us and ultimately it ruins our human values and our own character. The "trap of destruction" is so powerful that once we get into it, we are not able to differentiate what is right and wrong for us. And ultimately results in our own destruction.

Here is a learning and quick reference for this chapter: -

- Life is an ongoing journey between birth, death and rebirth.
- Our life is a roller-coaster. It continuously undergoes changes. Nothing is permanent in life, be it happiness, sadness, loneliness or pain, pain. It is like seasons that come and go.
- There is a difference between the physical body and the immoral soul that resides within the body. The body gets its power and energy from the soul. The physical body is temporary and undergoes continuous changes and destruction. The end of our physical body, we call death.
- However, from a spiritual lens, the soul just moves from one body to another. In simple words, the body takes different shapes and forms. And it is the accumulation of our karma (actions) that decides our fate in this birth as well as in all subsequent births that we take post our death.
- The more positive our karma, the better our life in terms of inner peace, happiness and satisfaction. We build our karmic accounts based on good and bad karma. And this karmic account and its debts continue in this birth and all subsequent births that we take post our death

- We must maintain a good positive balance so that we are freed up from past debt (from our previous life) and try to purify ourselves based on our actions. Once we are purified, we reach the Mukti also called liberation from death.

- The karmic bondage and past karmic debts are the main reason for our pain and grief in this life. Those who get it, get towards purifying and nullifying past debts. Those who do not get it gets attracted to physical possessions, greed, lust and attachments with a series of desires in life.

- God has given us this life or birth as we had wished for it to fulfill pending desires and also to make us realize our mistakes and purify ourselves. But it comes with the karmic bondages. You have to clear the past debt to enjoy the fruits of the present.

- Those born with good fortune, are the lucky ones with no past debts but due to their ignorance, they also start running towards accumulations, more and more physical possession, ultimately spoiling their current life and all future lives.

- With practice and control, we can limit our attraction to physical objects and limit our desires. There is no end to desires. It triggers greed, lust and anger and ultimately results in the destruction of a human

- We must start performing our duties with honesty, without any expectations, or without worry about the outcome. This is the only way to limit your desires and reach a state of nirvana

- We are trapped by our mind. If we understand the reasons for our pain and grief, we can make attempts to purify our actions with good deeds. We need a balanced mind and trust in God to make ourselves a better version of ourselves.

- Life is meant for purification. It is meant for Mukti or liberation. God wants each of us to get purified with our actions. There is a clear message that senses gratification traps us in the bondage of attachment and affection, so we must understand it and get away from it.

- Life is an opportunity to make it enriching, make it meaningful and useful enough to serve God and others, let's make some efforts in that direction too.

CHAPTER IV

Importance of Karma or Duties

Every human is bound or forced to perform duties. Nobody can remain inactive or without action, even for a moment. We are bound by mother nature (Prakriti) to do actions or get engaged in some karma. Without actions, we cannot even think of living or bringing food to the table for survival. The choices of karma are entirely personal. You are free to pick the karma that you like, love or aspire for. God has given us complete freedom here. If your karma does not give you an inner peace that directly implies something is wrong either with your actions or your choices in life or your karma itself. This is a very simple formula to assess our karma and our inner peace. Our karmas are in our hands but the results or outcomes from those karmas are not in our control. We must learn and accept this bitter truth of life. Even your good karma or current life need not guarantee you success or fulfill your desires. The results are not in our control, we must remind to ourselves from time to time.

Bhagavad Gita helps to clearly understand and differentiate between good and bad karma, its side effects, and how to get aligned towards the right karma for attaining inner peace. It helps us to make ourselves immune to the outcomes or the end results. Gita guides you to do selfless or nishkaam karma or desireless duties i.e., the duties without any expectations in return. Our traditional belief system is so hard-wired that we cannot think of living life without thinking of self-gain. In fact, our actions are driven only when we foresee or perceive something in return for us.

Our karmas are mostly driven based on our attachments, desires and expectations. And when things do not work or deliver the expected outcome as per our wish, we feel pain, misery, loneliness, frustrations and anger. This results in our stress, depression and mental instability. We are so sensitive to negative impulses, thoughts and emotions that we do not want to fight against them. We often forget that; we are responsible for our progress and devastation. It is much easy to blame someone else or find faults in others for our poor state of affairs. We must learn to accept ownership of our life for whatever we face in life. It is the results of the choices that we have made in our current life and our previous lives that are either rewarding or punishing us. Having said this, it does not mean we stop doing any kind of karma as it is not possible to stay inactive or passive for anyone for a longer time. Mother nature will force us to do something for survival.

Our life is mostly driven by what we want from it which is nothing but our changing desires from time to time. There is no end to our desires and that is the reason there is no end to our pain. It is a simple equation that we do not get it. We compare it with others on how and why others have everything. But fail to realize that our karmic results are nothing but the outcome at different stages of life that are rewarded by God. There is no partiality or prejudice here. There is no preferential treatment to anyone by God. Our existence and state of life are nothing but the end result of our karma. It became more important to understand and start practicing good karma which is without attachments and desires so that we get inner peace. The whole human sufferings are primarily due to our inability to understand the side effects and trap of attachments and desires in our life.

The only way to conquer this dilemma is with the power of the mind, intellect and repeated reminders to ourselves and by practicing self-discipline and control regularly. We all have choices in life. Our mind knows what is right and wrong for us. We know greed is bad, we know physical accumulations are not going to last forever, we know we are going to die someday, our relatives, family members and kin are going to die anytime and we also understand that everything is going to be left behind. However, in spite of all this wonderful knowledge and understanding, we ignore the reality of life, why? Because of the temporary or momentary pleasure that we get from accumulation, achievements and desires. We do not get inner peace (in spite of those momentary pleasures) as we are blindered by attachment and growing desires. We fail to understand the trap of desires in our life.

Let's look at how can we control our desires using the power of our mind and intellect to make attempts to do good karma/duties for attaining ultimate satisfaction and inner peach. This helps us to face any kind of situation in life.

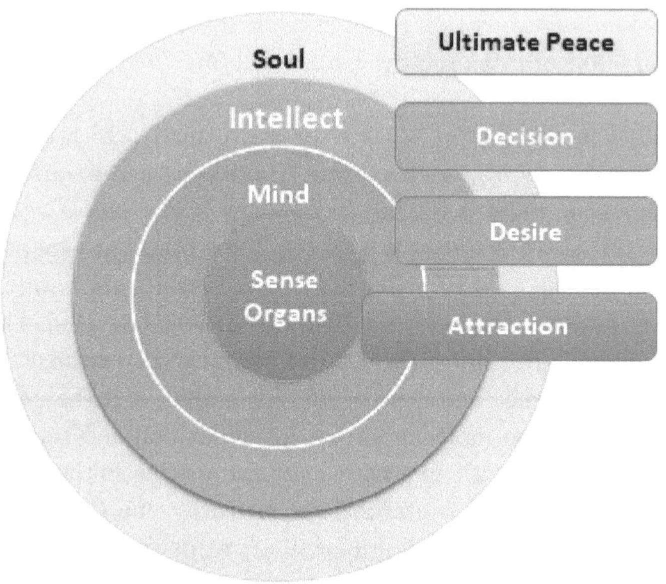

Trap of Life

Intelligence and stupidity have a very blurred line when it comes to understanding life. Many of us are stupid because we know greed, lust and attachments are bad things but we still chase them in our life. Real intelligence is knowing our boundaries and identifying factors that make us happy or sad and identifying how best to get ultimate peace in life. Bhagavad Gita makes it very clear that with attachments and growing desires no one can ever achieve peace in this life.

The Trap of mind is the simple correlation that links desires, sense organs, mind, intellect and peace. Our sense organs get attracted towards the subjects (attraction) which we like or aspire for in this world. This develops the attachment to subjects. It triggers a deep desire in our mind. Our intellect helps us to decide either to chase the desire or drop it. Intellect helps to differentiate between right and wrong. Since our decision-making process is mostly driven by our greed, lust, anger, revenge, jealousy etc, we tend to chase our desires most of the time. Our end goal is never the ultimate peace but rather our never-ending chase for accumulations and more and more expectations from life. This makes it obvious why we are never at peace or always worried. We are always hunting or chasing something things in life. Be it peace, be it accumulation, be it lusty affairs or other materialistic things. Those who are able to control their attraction to such physical objects of this world can limit their desires with the power of their mind and intellect. We must learn how to control our senses on various attractions to limit our desires.

Self-control helps us to detach from physical accumulation and limit our greed. In the worst case, even if you are not able to detach yourself completely, you can start preparing yourself to abort the shocks of life and learn to face failures strongly. The desires when gets fulfilled, it takes the form of greed. And when it is not fulfilled, takes the form of anger. In both cases, desires are harmful. With this Gita guidance, we can learn to control our desires and attachment. With this simple rule, our karma gets aligned to noble or selfless causes, as such activities are holy and peaceful in nature. We learn to understand that everything is temporary in this world and gifted by God so attractions and attachments are harmful. We get spiritual gradually with such a thinking process and start experiencing inner peace.

With the power of our mind, the understanding of materialistic things and their negative impacts on us become so clear that we either give up the materialistic attraction or start absorbing the shocks of failed outcomes in life with courage. Be it accumulation, relations or anything, we start accepting failures, defeats and losses with more mental strengths than ever. Our actions become our duties with the aim of helping ourselves and others. We start practicing good habits that are universal. We start getting detached from this physical world gradually over a period of time. Once we change our perception of life, we start believing in the power of God more than before and start experiencing peace. If there is peace within, everything that is materialistic outside looks insignificant. Our karma and karmic power understanding become so clear that we do everything for the almighty and get satisfied within. Let's start practicing the duties that are without attachment to purify ourselves. With the trust in God, this is possible. We need a belief in the beginning. Yes, there are no other preconditions for spirituality. The trap of life needs to be understood as soon as possible. With control of our mind and intellect, we can achieve inner peace. All we need is self-belief, self-control, trust in God and mental strengths to face the outcome and surprise of our life.

Here is a learning and quick reference for this chapter: -

- We cannot stay inactive or without any actions in our life. For survival, we are forced by mother nature to do some duties or perform actions.
- We have choices and freedom to pick good or bad duties. It is our ignorance and stupidity that distract us from performing noble duties and we get attracted to the physical accumulations and attachments in our life
- The temporary pleasure, sense of achievement and desires forces us to look at things that are materialistic in nature and develops the attraction
- It is our trap of mind that blurs our thinking to differentiate between right and wrong
- The attractions, desires, greed, anger, lust and peace are correlated. Our sense organs develop the attractions toward physical objects (materialistic gain) which triggers the desires and attachment
- Desires when gets fulfilled amplify further for more gain. When desires are not fulfilled it takes the form of anger. In both cases, desires are the reasons for our pain and suffering in life
- Each human is unique and has the influence of mother nature in different proportions. Few of us are spiritual, few are partially spiritual, few are greedy, few are lazy and few are cunning.
- Human behavior is driven by the influence of mother nature on each individual. The three nature qualities (Saat, Raaj and Taam) have ongoing changes and influence human life
- We change, our perceptive changes and our views towards life change throughout our life
- Those who are able to understand the above correlation, and develop self-discipline and self-control and such individuals are the ones who experiences peace and satisfaction in life
- The trap of life is due to poor coordination of sense organs, mind and intellect. When the mind and intellect are not able to control the senses (that triggers desires), we get attracted to matristic things
- With a balanced mind and power of intellect, we can limit our mind to differentiate what is needed for inner peace and ultimate satisfaction
- We must start practicing the habit to control our desires (by limiting our attractions). With trust in God, spiritual path and self-discipline we can definitely archive it
- With this, we can make ourselves immune to any shocks and surprises of life. Our duties get aligned towards the right things and we start experiencing the inner peace

CHAPTER V

The Power of Intelligence

The real intelligence of life is to understand the ongoing changes and challenges of life. Life will continue to give shocks and surprises to everyone. One can live it with fear, anger, frustrations and attachment. The other option is to face life as it comes without too much of botheration. This is real intelligence.

Even if you do not have any faith in God (atheist) but have the above mindset to face life with courage, you are living a Gita-driven life already. The only difference is what are you chasing in life and do you have inner peace? If it is not, then you need to change or adjust your perspective towards life to make it better.

Mother nature will continue to attract us to its creations which we call attractions. We are not talking about the greenery here. We are talking about possessions and materialistic things that develop greed in humans. How we exhibit the control in our life that defines our individuality. If one can make himself or herself immune to the shocks of nature, then such individuals are not influenced by anything in life. Be it a good or bad situation, profitable or loss-making scenario or temptation of life. One who is able to navigate life without attachment, fear, greed, anger, expectations and lust is as pure as God. But we are not God, so we all have shortcomings.

Now the question is about, do we really know what is the right thing to do, what we need to ignore and what we should not do? The answer would vary from person to person. Is there a standard approach that can make us pick between right and wrong? Definitely Yes! Bhagavad Gita makes it very clear and you can test it yourself.

We need to understand what kind of karma traps us in life and prevents our inner peace. This distinction can help us pick the right duties in life. We have the freedom to pick actions and duties. Few prefer not to get indulge in performing duties for fear of getting stuck into the karmic trap or getting into a conflict or bad karma. This is wrong thinking. Not indulging in karma in fear of being trapped is laziness or cowardness. But if you are not having any expectations from any duties or actions that you are performing, then such duties become divine. You should be neutral to the outcome and neutral to situations. We must devote all our duties as a social responsibility or service to God. The actions and outcomes that are devoted to God without self-interest are pure and give ultimate peace. Do not have any desires or expectations of your karma and devote your actions to God with sincere efforts. This is the ultimate state of intelligence and purifies us. With our powerful intellect, we can achieve it by limiting our senses, desires, lust, anger, greed and ego.

With a balanced mind and intellect, one can control our desires and expectations, limit our ego and can make ourselves immune to the end outcome or results. With such practice, we never get trapped into the karmic bondages and get freed from any kind of sins. We are just perming our duties with full devotion and efforts. This is what we need in life for a peaceful mind. Please understand the trap of mind is baked within our mind itself. You need intelligence to differentiate what is right and what is wrong for you for the ultimate life. Such thinking makes us focus on divine knowledge rather than materialistic attachments. Every action performed by an individual here becomes a sacrifice (to God) and people get freed from karmic bondage gradually.

As per Gita, sacrifice is the ultimate path to reaching salvation. You may call it the sacrifice of ego, the sacrifice of attachments, the sacrifice of greed, the sacrifice of lust, or the sacrifice of desires. Without sacrifice, there is no freedom from the karmic trap. We can never live a peaceful life without sacrifice. Few call it to sacrifice to God but in reality, it is your self-control, self-discipline and self-correction that is helping you alone to reach a superior state. God does not need anything from us. Period. The sacrifice helps us to purify our past karma, karmic bondage and make ourselves better human beings of today. Few donate their wealth or money as a sacrifice for purification, but such sacrifice is of no use if it is done with self-interest, for self-esteem, as self -propaganda or as a social show-off. Such actions are mere drama and can never give ultimate peace or happiness to anyone. Other types of sacrifices such as fasts, mantra chanting and holy pilgrimages all are fine, but if they are not performed with the ultimate objective of self-purification and inner peace are of little use or value.

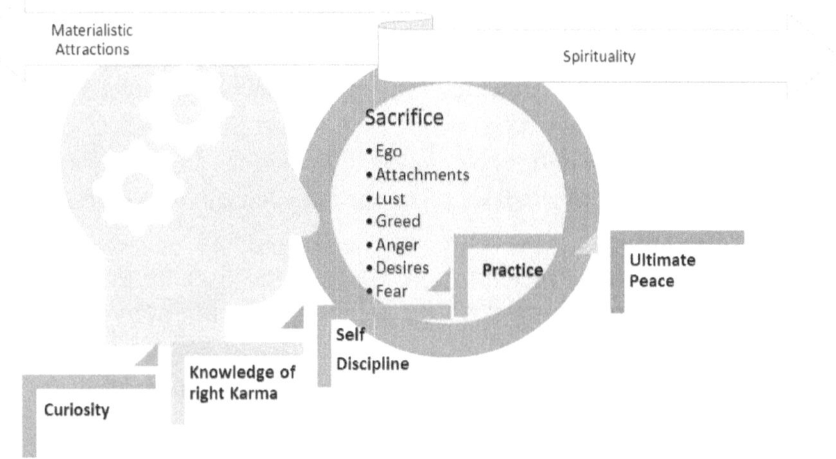

How our intelligence decides our material vs spiritual preferences

The sacrifice performed in knowledge is far superior to any material sacrifice. This makes our path to salvation easy. You need a teacher or a mentor who has practiced spiritual life and lived a self-less true living in case you find it too difficult to practice. One must find such a teacher who can make us realize some of these deep-rooted principles and realities of life which we ignore or take for granted in our life. Once we get this divine knowledge from our teacher or guru, we will never turn towards external attachments and attractions. This is because the divine knowledge will enforce our belief that all living beings are the same and portion or part of the same Almighty.

The divine knowledge burns our ego and ignorance, and any reactions or attractions from the materialistic world are also burnt similar to the wood that is turned into ashes by the fire. There is nothing purer than the divine knowledge in this entire universe. With devotion and faith in God, we can attain this knowledge during this life itself at the right time. And this gives the ultimate peace.

The person who possesses neither the faith nor the knowledge, and who is of doubting nature, suffers a downfall. For the skeptical or suspicious soul, there is no happiness either in this life or the next. One must cut the doubts and ignorance with the sharpness of knowledge and make every effort to make life meaningful.

Here is a learning and quick reference for this chapter: -

- We all are free to make choices. While we may control our choices in life, we do not control the outcome. This implies that our choice or actions are important in life
- The karma we pick defines our actions. Our actions are mostly driven by our self-interest and when we do not get an adequate result, we feel pain or anger
- We must identify what kind of karma traps us, gives us pain and what can make us immune and strong to any kind of karma without hurting or harming anyone.
- Bhagavad Gita clearly guides us to use our intellect to control choices we make, and control/refrain from actions that are counterproductive
- It guides us to gain the knowledge that can free us from external stimulus, attraction, pain, sufferings, greed, anger and all possible negativities in life
- In this life, we often suffer due to our karmic bondage and debts of our karma. This needs some sacrifice which is not that difficult to practice. It needs the sacrifice of ego, the sacrifice of anger, the sacrifice or greed, the sacrifice of attachment and the sacrifice of desires
- With devotion and faith in God, one can attain divine knowledge. If you still feel it is not practical, then find a guru or teacher who had been practicing it and living a selfless life.
- Why do you care for it? The simple reason being you are not at peace; you are in constant pain and suffering. And we need it badly because materialistic things give us pain.
- There is no easy route here as mother nature will continue to attract us towards its shining, greedy, materialistic things and the society around us will measure our progress or success based on our accumulations. We have to make a conscious choice here.
- You can continue to accumulate till the last day of death, still, we will never be at peace. This implies the peace is somewhere else and we are chasing something wrong in life
- These aspects are well stated in Vedic scriptures thousands of years ago and it also guides us to practice spirituality for peace of mind. And it delivers results. You may call it the scientific method or faith or spirituality. It does not matter; you just need a start to make your life enriching.

- This is similar to doing exercise, we know, we need to be regular and committed, otherwise there are no results. The same is true with spirituality. We need to develop it.
- The divine knowledge burns our ego and ignorance, and any reactions or attractions from the materialistic world are also burnt similar to the wood that is turned into ashes by the fire.
- There is nothing purer than the divine knowledge in this entire universe. With devotion and faith in God, we can attain this knowledge during this life itself at the right time.

Choosing the right Karma

As a human, we are confused about what kind of karma we should do or which are suitable for us. We have seen many saints and sages around us who have been worshiping in remote locations. Few of us call them fake. Few of us worship them and few of us observe them. As a human, we all are different and so are our actions and beliefs. So, what is right and wrong? What kind of karma can give inner peace?

As per Bhagavad Gita, we have the freedom to pick our karma. Every karma gets us into bondage. The bondage of desires and outcomes or results. We cannot live without performing karma as for survival we need to do something in this world. There are many saints who have given up the materialistic attractions and they find peace in deep mountains and caves. We cannot live such hard life. But in reality, living a karmic life with doing your duties in the materialistic world by facing different situations, different people, and different relations are much more difficult than living a saint alike life in an isolated jungle or mountain. Yes, this is true. One form of karma is called Karma Sanyash (Sanyash refers to giving up karma that creates bondage in life), the other is called Karmayog (doing regular karma however filtering the wrong or bad karma that traps us or gives us pain). Both paths take us towards liberation.

We must understand that we can attain inner peace through both paths (Path of Karma Yoga and Path of Karma Sanyash). One path is by living the regular life which we all are already in today and the other one is living the spiritual sage alike lifestyle in a deep jungle or bank of a river or inside caves away from common people. Both paths can give us liberation. The reason the saints or sages preferred remote locations is primarily to isolate themselves from the distracting world, distracting attachments, subjects and relationships. They also face severe hardship and in fact many of them return back to regular life after facing the hard life in mountains, jungles and caves. Life is not easy for anyone; be it you, me or a saint. So what matters is how we make ourselves immune to situations, how we pick the right things and how we attain the peace within.

By now, you must have realized, why we need inner peace. All our pains and griefs are because of the poor state of mind within. The external matristic things, cannot give permanent peace. Ask a billionaire or a millionaire if he or she is really at peace? The answer would certainly be No.

The people who are real karma yogis are the ones who have controlled their senses, mind and intellect and view everyone as the same across the world. Yogi refers to the one who sacrifices. The sacrifice is of desires, greed, lust, anger and every bad quality that traps us in this materialistic world. The people who do not get trapped into the worldly bondage of desires, lust and greed is the one who experiences peace in reality. Such people are not attracted or distracted by the outcome and end results. They have isolated themselves from the shocks of life. They have faith in God. And they do every action for God or at least devote it to God. And whatever they get (gain), they devote themselves to God. They do not have the ego of "I", "Me", or "My". Rather for them, everything belongs to God and they prefer to devote it back to God in case the world gives them something. They do not have the ego of "I am the doer". They are not influenced by the attachment and gain in this materialistic world.

You must be thinking. They are like a saint. And such things are difficult to practice. Yes, you are right. It is a very difficult path and there is only a minuscule population here in this entire world. However, the whole world is gradually moving or wants to move towards the spiritual path. The path of inner peace where we purify ourselves, our karma. And someday, if we are lucky, we reach there. But people have started experiencing deep inner peace even though they may not have reached 100% there yet. The spiritual path once traversed, gives deep inner peace that can be felt and experienced. Spirituality is practiced in every religion. The methods or names could be different but the underlying concept is to purify yourselves. When our every action gets aligned towards the purification of self, we automatically detach ourselves from this materialistic world. The relations and materialistic things that hurt us are the reasons why we are trapped in this world. And the reasons for our sufferings.

The idea is not to become a saint here. With our regular life also, we can attain divine peace or at least can experience it with practice. All we need to do is to perform our duties with honesty, with a balance of mind and intellect and give up the expectations or the results. The results are anyways not in our control so why feel concerned or worried about it.

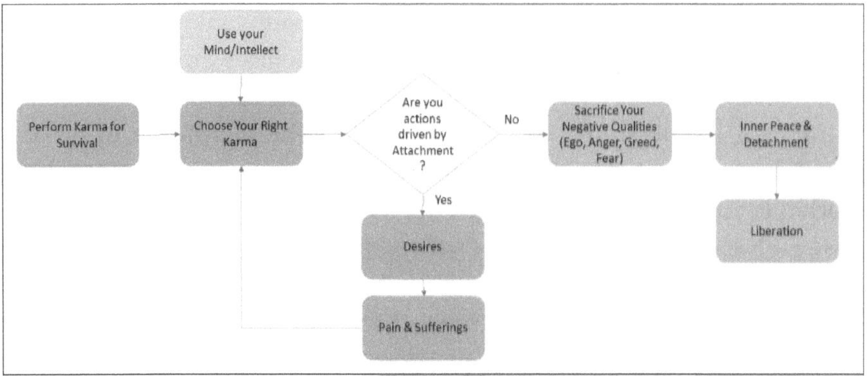

Karma Cycle of Pain, Suffering and Liberation

We need a method to convince our noisy minds. And spirituality is the best answer here. Once we develop faith in the Almighty and devote all our actions and outcomes to God, we are already mid-way on the liberation path. We must look at everyone with a common lens of humanity and adjust our actions. Once we start developing sympathy for every creature of the universe (plants, animals, humans, living or non-living things), we transition into the divine state of liberation. Our actions get aligned automatically. We must connect with God. Once we start doing it, we experience peace. And his state (when we are immersed in spiritual thoughts or meditation) does not distract us from the materialistic world and a ray of peace emerges within automatically. Such individuals who experience inner peace are not bothered about happiness, gain, loss or anything else. They are in a peaceful state where the mind is at peace. One such mastery is developed; our focus automatically shifts to the spiritual side (away from the materialistic things). Such masters of spiritual knowledge, are the same in every situation and their trust and faith in God do not deplete under any circumstances.

The happiness that we experience due to materialistic gain or due to our senses, although gives a feel-good feeling, in reality, it is temporary and the real reason for our pain and suffering. Intelligent people do not get trapped in the materialistic things (gain or loss) of this world. The one who strives to contain the anger, desires and lust and conquer them, is the one who experiences real peace in this world. And this is the ultimate liberation stage where we have only connected with the Almighty, our actions are for God, and the rest all is secondary to us including our pain and sufferings. The one who believes that God is the supreme power, the giver, the provider, and the caretaker of everyone, is the one who experiences inner peace.

Here is a learning and quick reference for this chapter: -

- For a happy and peaceful life, we need a method to find out why we are not at peace? The answers lie within us and the choices we make in our life
- The only person responsible for the poor state of our mind or poor state of our life is each of us. We as an individual should take the blame for our destruction, not the external world or people around us or the circumstances whom we often blame for our poor state
- A saint is also struggling to get peace and the same is our situation. Saint moves from jungles to mountains to caves to find peace whereas we chase it in form of materialistic gain and relationships in our lives
- We can attain peace by both the path of Karmayog and KarmaSanyash. One is the path of living and facing the world, other is to move away from the physical world away and perform union with God for ultimate peace
- Both paths demand sacrifice. The sacrifice of desires, greed, attachments, anger, lust, and physical gain
- The physical gain cannot give us peace. It triggers and aggravates our greed further. And we get more attracted towards physical possession, be it wealth, money or its other forms. We get selfish, angry and egoistic
- Life is all about the choices we make. The physical attractions and materialistic gain can only give pain. This is universally accepted. Spirituality is the answer. For ultimate peace, we need to focus on the right things that can give us ultimate peace.
- We must pick the karma that does not trap us into the bondage of desires, greed, attachments and anger. Our action should be towards the purification of self. Once we attempt here, we are making a start on the liberation path.
- With trust in God and practice, we can attain inner peace and purify ourselves by living a karmayogi life. Spirituality is the ultimate destination for attaining peace and mediation is one of the first steps to getting there.
- With the right karma, we can attain liberation. We need not change ourselves or our existing life dramatically. All we need is a bit of control over our mind so that it guides us to focus on the right things that are

useful for us.

- We are already doing many karmas or actions every day. All we need is to absorb the shocks of output or material gain in life and gradually make ourselves neutral to the situations or circumstances. If such things still give pain, we can start distracting our mind to something peaceful activities

- It is all about how we manage our mind. We should avoid the trap of mind which gets us into the trap of destruction as we have seen in the earlier chapters. With the power of intelligence, we can pick the right karma that does not put us into bondage in this world. And once our karma gets aligned, life comes back on track.

CHAPTER VII

Managing Disappointments: Understanding our Mind

In the earlier chapter, we have learned the importance of inner peace and how to attain it. In this chapter, we will learn why we are not at peace? We must learn some basics of how our mind operates, how our desires develop, and how we react to situations and circumstances from time to time. Depression, anger, frustrations and challenges come in everyone's life just that different people react or handle them differently. You must have seen few people always in a happy mood whereas few are always distressed, disappointed with life, and under the attack of depression. This is not about the theory of handling negative emotions, but more about understanding our mind which can be our greatest friend as well as greatest enemy.

We need to assess if our mind is behaving as our friend or enemy. This needs regular self-check-up similar to our health check-ups. Those who understand the strengths and weaknesses of their mind, know how best to convince themselves in different situations. Those who have conquered their mind, can face any situations. Determination, hope, patience and never giving up are not just big jargon, but they do have significance when it comes to how our mind reacts to different situation in our life. We must elevate the power of our mind so that we become powerful mentally. Yes, mental inner peace is more powerful than any other rewards one can experience. Let's look at the mind closely. We already read about the medical significance of the mind, amygdala, hormone secretion, and its impact on our mental health in the first chapter, now let's look at it from the spiritual lens.

Our mind operates at 4 different levels. Many of us have come across some of the keywords as shown in the picture below, either English or Sanskrit. We are referring to Maan, Buddhi, Chitta, and Ahankaar (i.e., **Mind, Intellect, Attachment and Ego**). These are not 4 different things but the same aspect of the mind that acts or operates differently to different stimuli or impulses or inputs. We must learn to understand at which level, the mind is dominant within us. Once we get it, we can assess if it is harming us or helping us. Let's understand it closely.

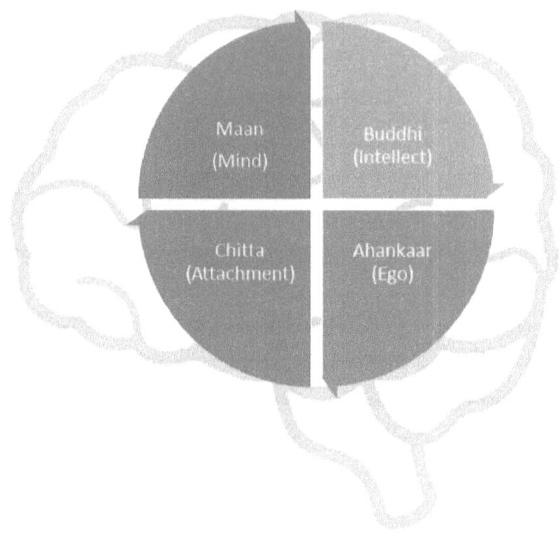

Four levels of our Mind

- **Maan/Mind**: When our mind creates thoughts, we call it Maan or the mind
- **Buddhi/ Intellect**: When the mind analyses and decides, we call it Buddhi or intellect
- **Chitta/Attachment**: When it gets attached to any object, we call it Chitta.
- **Ahankaar/Ego**: When we feel proud of objects such as wealth, status, beauty, learning, etc, it is referred to as ahankara or our ego

Someone who feels low, demotivated, or distressed finds out which mind layer is operating at then within them. The negative thoughts of the mind often dilute or weaken our intellectual thinking and energy and we often make wrong choices or wrong decisions. Never operate your mind too much under the influence of Chitta (when we are under self-doubts, fear, or under affection); the negativity originates indirectly from Chitta and Ahankaar (when you are overconfident or make judgements without facts, etc). These lead to pain and suffering that ultimately give negative stress and are the reasons for depression in many.

We need to balance our Maan and Buddhi for living this peaceful life. Bhagavad Gita indicates that we must elevate positive thoughts so that we can leverage or sharpen our intellect (buddhi) effectively. Otherwise, we often harm ourselves either physically, mentally or emotionally. The emotional hijack happens when our mind is over-influenced by our Chitta (attachments) and Ahankaar (Ego). We must strengthen our mind so that it operates more with intellect rather than with Chitta and Ahankaar. Spirituality can help to overcome the influence of Chitta and Ahankaar. It helps you to focus on the right thing and can calm down your brain activities completely.

We can control our thinking with positive or negative thoughts. Our thought (s) serves as input (breakfast) in our decision-making. This is universally accepted. There is a need to think positive for a reason. The simple explanation is when you are thinking too negatively or only the negatives, the decision layer of the mind (i.e., our intellect) is going to pick from those set of thoughts (read it as negative thoughts). The intellect is bound to operate on those negative thoughts (from the set of various inputs you have given to it) and often the result is negative. And in all probability, you are going to hurt or harm yourself negatively when you think negatively. This is simple input-> process-> output equation. If the input is faulty, the output cannot be positive.

Let's analyze why people get thoughts of killing themselves a little deeper. Such individuals, when hammered by poor life situations or a series of bad experiences, give up hopes in this world. When they are in an extremely poor state of mind, their mind triggers, severe series of negative thoughts such as "what is the use of such life?" "The world is not fair to them", "They are worthless", "they cannot face it anymore" etc. Unfortunately, such people are so depressed that they are not able to take a pause or take guidance. They need help but very few get it timely. And when such people send various non-stopping negative thoughts to their intellect, the intellect, assesses the series of all negative thoughts, and looks for any valid reasons for living a life. The intellect, unfortunately, picks up the strongest negative thought that dominates in mind in such a situation. Quite often, for few people, the attachment and ego thoughts in mind may help stop them from taking drastic decisions.

The attachment could be the memory of their relatives or someone whom they still care for and love or the person who had been kind to them in their life. The mixed emotions get triggered and the person's thought process abruptly gets interrupted by the impulse of attachment or the ego. And the decision process of negative processing of intellect stops with emotional thoughts. One must stop negative thinking and stop taking any drastic decisions that put their lives in danger. Life is beautiful and the journey of life never ends, even after we try to give up our current life.

After our death, we are answerable to God. God would like to know why someone killed themselves when they had a life to live and purify themselves while facing the world. And the next birth post reincarnation could be more severe or painful if we are not determined to face the hard situations or hardships in our current life. Our soul never gets peace when someone ends their life abruptly. This is the truth in spirituality. One must learn to face life irrespective of situations in life. Positivity definitely works and influences our life no matter whatever may be our belief system.

One must feed with positive thoughts to mind regularly. If you cannot do it, at least try to either distract your mind (e.g., listen to music, exercise, swim, play, walk in nature, etc) or get focused (e.g., meditation). These aspects, at least, help minimize or neutralize the impact of negative thinking within our noisy minds.

There is a reason, the whole literature and intellects talk about positive thinking, positive attitude, and looking positive side of life. Bhagavad Gita clearly tells that when you have no one to go after or there is no one you believe in, you can look at God for help. And you will get the blessings of God in some form in this life. Have some faith or belief. Without it, life is meaningless. We must make ourselves immune to the situations, be it good or bad. The power of mind must be used in a manner that helps elevate ourselves. We must focus on God or the superpower whom we believe regularly.

The unfortunate state of many people in today's world is that when they are in real pain or grief, only then remember God for seeking help. Other times, they hardly care or do not practice the worship regularly. We are selfish with God as well as per our needs or as per our pain. One must change such attitude and start practicing good acts and deeds. One must work towards the purification of Maan (Mind) and try to make ourselves strong to face any situation in life. We must feel the extreme pleasure of connecting with God. This is called Yog, the union with God. This is different from Yoga which is more of a physical fitness program. The "Yog" in spirituality is nothing but connection or union with God.

Bhagavad Gita makes it clear that you need continuous practice and detachment from the physical world to connect with God. "No expectations in return", Zero attachment, and a neutral and fearless mind are the basic foundation which we must learn. When we develop such qualities, we treat everyone with equality. With this virtue, one can feel or experience the existence of God in everyone, every creature, and every living and non-living thing.

This is difficult but if we need real spiritual peace in life, we can make some attempts here. Mediation is one of the ways that can help you connect with yourself and God within you and around you. We need to develop the focus and trust in God to conquer our biased thinking or selfish motto in life. Once we develop such an ability to connect or focus on God (either through yog or meditation or some other methods), we become situations neutral, relationship neutral and live a spiritual life. This does not mean you give up your relationship, duties or your routine activities in life. The Karmayog is essential and cannot be given up by anyone.

One must develop abilities to train the mind to give up all desires, impact of any situation, the impact of any shocks in life, and other qualities that make us impure with impurities such as anger, lust, greed and ego. Connecting with self is an indirect way of connecting with God. And when we train our mind to start believing and practicing such aspects, we make an attempt to start living a spiritual life which is the purest life that God expects from us. We must relate everything to God and thank him for everything in our life.

God is not responsible for our success or failure; it is purely owned by each of us and our actions. So, when we take credit or anything, we must take the blame as well. One cannot blame God for the poor state of their life. You need to find ways to purify yourselves, your deeds and your journey towards liberation. Bhagavad Gita clearly says that with practice and detachment it is possible to attain this. All you need is a start and the rest all will fall in place automatically either in this birth or the other subsequent births that we may take post our death. Those who trust God and think of God all the time in their mind (in spite of being indulged in social activities or regular affairs of life are the ones who are liked the most by God. The mind is playing the mind-games with us, so we must use it wisely. Let's manage our thoughts to handle disappointments and shocks in life. And train our mind for such things. Disappointments and shocks are inevitable in life for anyone, all we need is a method to absorb them and keep moving!

Here is a learning and quick reference for this chapter: -

- There is a popular saying that "one must learn enough about the enemies before fighting with them". This applies to our mind too. Our mind can be our best friend as well as our biggest enemy
- We must learn how we behave in different situations. Understanding our mind is essential to dealing with failure, disappointments and shocks of life. Those who have conquered their mind to handle such aspects can face any tough situations.

- Bhagavad Gita makes us understand that we should be situation agnostics and face the world. We must monitor our emotions and different level of mind which includes: Maan, Buddhi, Chitta and Ahankaar (i.e., **Mind, Intellect, Attachment and Ego**)
- Filtering out negative thoughts and negative feelings is not only important but is a must condition for us to fight back with situations, face the world and its extremities
- Those who are mentally weak in terms of handling negative thinking or feelings, face an extreme state of disappointments and failures in life. Such individuals must learn the power of positivity, understand how the mind operates and they must develop connections with God i.e., they need spiritual connections to elevate them and empower themselves. God does not expect anything from anyone, so there is no harm to make him your true friend.
- While spirituality can help anyone, people who are vulnerable to impulses, shocks, negativity and surprises must practice spirituality which is nothing but connecting with self and with the God that exists within each of us in our hearts.
- One must start believing in God that gives us strengths to face the extremes of life. You need continuous practice and detachment from the physical world to connect with God.
- When we limit our desires or expectation from life, we indirectly cut ourselves from aftershocks of failures, disappointments and surprises of life.
- With a belief in our mind, we can align our mind towards God and gradually can cut ourselves from the external attractions and can develop a connect with the God

- Let's make the best use of our mind with positivity to make an attempt towards our liberation journey. Even if you do not get liberation immediately, you will feel light, relaxed and motivated.

41

CHAPTER VIII

The illusion of Maya

Many of us are familiar with the word "Maya". It is the illusion that manifests things that are not real or are the temporary one. The Maya is not bad. Yes, you read it right. It is the purest form of power of God. Maya helps us get to the things that we desire or aspires for in our life. Many of us desire money, wealth, accumulations, position, power, relationship, love, etc and Maya helps us achieve it. But the more we tilt towards the physical possessions of the world; the more we go away from God. In short, our pain and suffering are primarily due to us running for things that are illuminated by Maya. The Maya is also referred to as material energy. This energy is superior to our soul energy and that is the reason we dance to the tune of the Maya.

Maya sits in between God and us. Those who are in real search of God do not aspire for anything material but rather desires union with God. Moment, we surrender ourselves to God, the power of Maya which is a materialistic illusion gets transparent and we can see and experience God. In such a case, Maya helps us to achieve God or attain God. This is the state of intellectual supremacy. And this happens when we realize that real peace is when we surrender ourselves and everything to God.

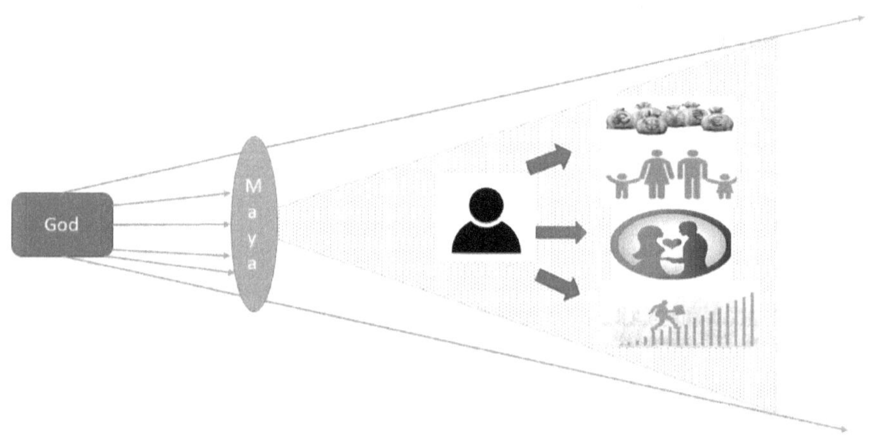

Maya and its influence on us

God has given us choices and freedom to pick either himself or his power which is the Maya. Many of us run towards the Maya due to our ignorance. Very few understand that the real master is the God and not the Maya. Maya is the power of God and indirectly acts as a slave to God and follows every instruction of God. God is the only superpower. Maya is doing her duties towards the god. Maya has created every materialistic object in the world that is temporary.

Maya develops bondages in humans. The desire for money, love, relationship, family, success, etc all are driven because of the illusion and illumination created by Maya. Maya keeps testing us so that we can understand the difference between the Truth (God) and illusion (materialistic things). The awareness and intelligence help us develop this knowledge which is spirituality. Spirituality helps to pick the divine things. It makes our focus clear. It clears our ignorance. It encourages us to surrender to God, not because of any fear or power difference but primarily due to love, respect, and affection for God.

Bhagavad Gita makes it very clear that the ultimate supreme power is God and without awareness, raising our knowledge, and surrendering to God, we cannot get God or its blessings. We have a choice in our life so in end it is each of us who is accountable for our pain and suffering. We cannot blame others or God or someone else for our actions and choices in life.

One must be wondering, why God gives us pain, grief, and suffering. This is not true. Our pains are due to our choices and decisions. This is due to our ignorance. People often make fun of the word "Maya" or talk intellectually about it but still chase worldly possessions (and suffer pain in end). Irrespective of the religion we follow, we already know that we have a temporary life in this world. So, whatever we get in life or achieve here, is temporary. Everything is owned by mother nature and we have just inherited things for a short time (as long as we live) and we must give them back.

We are not the owner but rather a tenant in this life. While we know, that the moment we die, everything will remain here in mother nature only, still, we chase things. This is primarily because of our fear. We think we should accumulate things so that when we have a real hard time, we do not suffer or face hardship and we build some cushion or backup. But in reality, our sufferings are primarily due to our desires and greed. That will never get fulfilled in this life and any subsequent life that we may take after our death. Those who get it, are the one who starts practicing a spiritual life that gives them peace of mind. Let's not blame God for our poor state of mind and our poor choices in life.

The Almighty has always been kind to us and helped us achieve what we aspire for. Be it physical accumulations in form of money, wealth, relationship, family, power, etc. However, God has also made it clear in Bhagavad Gita that all of these are not good things but a trap for attachment, And the primary cause of grief and pain. We have seen in earlier chapters how our mind can be our friend as well as our enemy. God will continue to fulfill our desire (in this material world) for what we aspire for if we work hard irrespective of the religion we follow. Hard work is rewarded but it comes with a caveat that such reward is temporary. God has its eternal existence and presence everywhere as well as within every creature across universes.

We often get confused with unmanifested form and manifested form of God. God has always existed in both of these forms (form as well as formless). We need to be in a divine state to witness God and experience his presence. That means we need to either be in our purest form so that we can experience him. Or we need his blessings to get his spiritual union. Without any of these two things, we cannot attain God.

God has empowered Maya to take care of us. She is the one who takes part in the creation of this universe and every creature within it, every material in it. And she is executing things as per the order of the Almighty. She is the producer of every creature. Like any mother, she helps her children (read it as all of us) fulfill our dreams, including fulfilment of our greed, desires, power, etc. But she also punished us and gives us hard lessons about life from time to time so that we can improve. When we are not ready to give up wrong things (read them as materialistic things), she forcefully takes them away from us.

Just imagine the situation, when you have lost your precious things, relatives, or relationship with someone. Maya wants us to understand that everything is temporary and illusionary. This indicates nothing is permanent including this universe. Even it undergoes destruction. So why worry about things if we lose something, no matter how precious it may be. It does not belong to us anyway. We are just the temporary possessor of things, so better prepare to get rid of things or make ourselves strong the face the impact of loss in our life. This is the hard reality. Everything is expected to finish or end and it happens as per the wish of the Almighty.

The power of God is beyond our imagination. As per Bhagavad Gita, God is the source of the entire creation, and when the world ends, everything dissolves into God. God is the taste of water, the radiance of sun and moon. He is the life force that is within each of us. Hindus call it "Aatma", the holy soul that is within our body which is keeping us alive in form of life energy. God is the intelligence, the glory, strength, and anything and everything that one can think of. God is the ultimate supreme energy. Those who surrender themselves to God and worship God are very dear to him.

Surrender does not mean; you give up everything and become a saint or sanyasi or inactive. Many do not get it and few make fun of spirituality. The simple explanation is that one must align every action either for the service to God or to humanity. The purpose of this life is to make ourselves as pure as God so that when we leave this life, we can match the purity of God so that we attain liberation. Liberation is freedom from the cycle of birth and death. This may not happen in one life and we may have to take other lives to get there. In end, God wants us to get pure, period! And he will continue to punish us till we improve. There is no other literature on this entire world, that can explain these things with Clarity. Bhagavad Gita teaches us a way of life.

We must also understand that without belief, surrender and devotion, we will never move to the path of spirituality. The illusion of Maya will continue to distract us. The reason is simple, Maya wants to test us again and again so that we become strong, attachment-free, desire free and devoted to God (to develop purity). Maya attracts us with its 3 qualities or Gunas i.e., Satva, Rajo and Tamo. These Gunas will influence us continuously in our life. One person in thousands infers such knowledge and a very few amongst those intellectuals continue to make God their ultimate destination and make attempts there. Our sufferings make us stronger. We must learn from our sufferings and challenges and convince our mind that there are valid reasons for our pain in this world. If we channel our mind into spirituality, we can become better human beings. Maya will help us either change our path toward God or will make us struggle in this temporary world due to its illusion. We must apply our mind and intellect to get the answer. The choice is entirely ours.

Here is a learning and quick reference for this chapter: -

- Maya is the power of God (few call it Goddess too) that teaches us the lessons of life from time to time

- It sits between us and God and attracts us towards its possessions, the material gain. The attachments, desires, greed, etc are being triggered due to our attraction to Maya
- One can either get Maya or God. You cannot get both. Maya gives pain, sufferings but the aim is to teach us lessons of life. Maya also develops our devotion and trust towards God by giving us shocks of life from time to time.
- Moment, we surrender ourselves completely to God, Maya guides us to develop purity. This in turn develops our inclination towards spirituality. However, such a path is very difficult
- One must understand that the primary reasons for our pain and suffering are due to our attachments to the Maya-driven objects. The ultimate peace is when we change our direction toward God. This is a paradigm shift in thinking. Our mind can help here.
- We have complete freedom and God has given us choices to pick what we desire. But we have to be ready to face the consequences of it too.
- Maya is an illusion in the world or its physical objects and possessions which are temporary. She herself is not bad as she is the supreme power of God and doing her duties towards the God

Maya originated from God and in end, she gets dissolved into God. The one who understands and realizes it makes the right choice in picking between God or Maya created objects

CHAPTER IX

Understanding Death, Next Life and Liberation

Death is the ultimate reality. We all have a temporary life which we often assume is up to 100 years. But it can be shorter too. The mortality rate differs in each country, each state and each city. There are thousands of people who die every day because of sudden death due to accidents, illness and other reasons. We all are afraid of death. It is a painful experience. Few of us may have witnessed it in the forms of the demise of our close relatives, family members and others. We do not want to talk about death because we think is not a good topic but if you look at it from a spiritual lens, it is an opportunity to attain liberation with ease. We need to know how part of it. And Bhagavad Gita teaches us it very beautifully.

Everything is temporary in this world including our lives. We need to remind ourselves of this fact repeatedly so that we are prepared to die and leave everything anytime. This helps absorb shocks better. Our family members, friends, spouse and kids all are going to die someday either before or after us. If we are prepared to accept that every relationship in life is temporary, we can feel lesser pain when any of our dear ones depart this world. This is more about training our mind to that we can absorb any shocks in life. We must also understand that only the physical body of an individual dies with the death, not the soul. The soul is ever-lasting. One must learn how to die with dignity. Yes, you read it right. Death is a very painful experience but one can practice making it lesser painful or even painless. The simple solution is to remember and pray to the Lord Supreme at the last minute of life when you leave this world. Such a simple solution, to attain Moksha or liberation.

However, one in a few million, get this right. People hardly pray to God during the last moment of life. The reason being we are not used to praying to God regularly. We are not thankful to God regularly. We do not remember him regularly, so when the time comes to leave this world, we remember everything else (which is materialistic) but not God. People often recall their relations, wealth, pain, suffering, and fear during the time of death. This is a natural phenomenon; we can recall only those things which we utter or remember most during our lives. Attachment, desires, greed and lust are the only aspects we chase, utter, think and practice during our entire life. And when the time comes to say goodbye to this world, we cannot only think outside these things or their related aspects.

The feeling, memory and thoughts that one gets at the time of death, decide our next life. Our rebirth is inevitable if we are not thinking or praying about God during the time of death. This is the ultimate truth from lord Krishna, which is clearly stated in Bhagavad Gita. We must utter the word "Om or Aum or ॐ" (the divine and holy word/symbol of God which is the primordial sound of the universe that represents the cosmic vibrations). By uttering "Aum" we are aligning our energy(soul) with the absolute cosmic energy (energy of God). One must remember or recall the lord supreme at the time of death so that liberation can be achieved. We must practice praying to God regularly, surrounding ourselves with God's company regularly so that we develop devotion and the thought to remember God comes naturally to us without any trigger. Practice makes us perfect and devotion to God comes with practice, not by chance.

The aim of our life is to purify ourselves. Very few of us get it correctly so we miss purifying ourselves due to various reasons and God cannot give us liberation due to our impurities. And that is the reason, rebirth is inevitable for many of us. The karma of this life is carried forward to the next life and we get either reward or punishment (read it as karmaphal) based on our karma. This is a cyclic process. Very simple to understand. The only way to purify ourselves is to surrender to God completely and he will take care of the rest. We need not worry about death or liberation or anything of that sort once we believe in God. Devotion to God is the only way to attain liberation and there are no shortcuts here. God controls every action of ours so even if someone wants to remind himself or herself to utter "Om" or "pray to God" at the time of death, it may not come naturally. We cannot fool God or take a shortcut to liberation.

One may ask, what is liberation and why it is important. The simple answer is: it is the path to free yourself from the pain and suffering forever. It is the freedom from the cycle of birth-death and rebirth. It is also called Mukti or real freedom. We all take millions of births and rebirths as per our deeds. Each life is full of pain, suffering and punishments. How long does one want to face it? Unless we purify ourselves with our karma, the rebirth is inevitable and we can take rebirth in any form such as plants, inspects, animals and other creatures. Very few get the rebirth as a human.

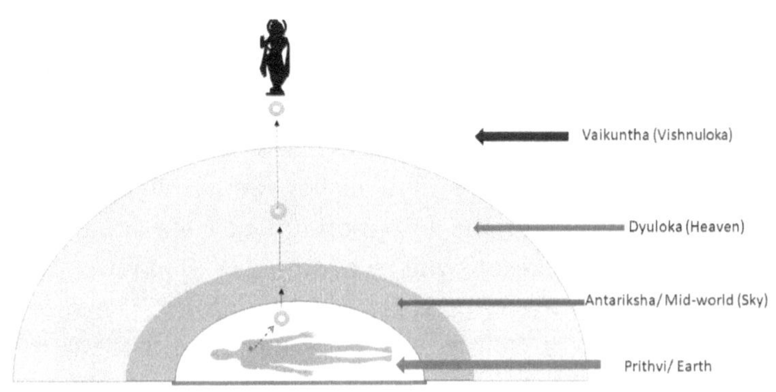

Journey of our soul: Path to Liberation

Just image yourself as an inset or a bird or animal and correlate to their life. Do you really want to get into that form or live such hard life, full of hardship on the earth? Many of us would say no to it. so, if you want freedom from such a life, liberation is the only way. Liberation is the simple union with the supreme Almighty forever.

Liberation is the union of the soul energy with the Eternal energy of God. The soul once leaves the earth, may either move upwards or downwards. The downward journey indicates the degradation of the soul whereas the upward movement of the soul indicates the upgrade of the soul into higher Loka/abodes. The Lord supreme is present adobe is called as Vaikunth a.k.a. the Vishnuloka. A pure soul can unite with the Almighty via the Anriksha (sky) and the Dyuloka (heaven). People who have mixed karma in their life, enjoy the higher Loka (e.g., stay in Heaven) for some time and when their positive karma results vanish or nullify, they are brought back to the earth to face the hardships. The purity of humans is a must factor for attaining the god.

We all know the level of our purity to some extent. Many of us are very impure too, so either be ready to face the outcome or consequence or surrender to God. The simple method is to surrender. God is very kind to everyone and takes care of everyone too. However, there are strict rule books that he follows when it comes to punishments. Each punishment of God is an opportunity to correct our mistakes, purify ourselves and service others. If we get these basics right, we can change our paradigm and viewpoints towards the world and others.

The place, time and date of our death are also prefixed when we take birth in this world. God has made all the arrangements already. We all have to go through the phases of happiness, sadness, aging, disease and death during our lifetime. It is up to us how we take it. One can either stay disappointed with life or has an option to enjoy life and devote it to the service of others. The results will be reviewed by God post our death. And rebirth or salvation would be granted as we qualify. The very important lesson from Bhagavad Gita is to do your duties, do not worry about the outcome, and leave the results to God. So, there is no need to worry about death or liberation or anything alike. We must do our duties keeping God as our main focus and ultimate destination. Things will fall in place.

We must take some time out and devote ourselves to God. We are not as busy as God, we are not as powerful and prosperous as God, we must thank him from time to time and pray and devote ourselves to him for such a beautiful life. Let's use this life meaningfully. Let's even use death as an opportunity to meet God and cut ourselves from all sufferings in our next lives. Let's devote ourselves and start our spiritual journey. It is never late for anything when we start it fresh. Trust in God, he will take care of the rest. Let's make death an enriching experience, not a painful experience.

Here is a learning and quick reference for this chapter: -

- Death is the reality of life and we must accept it and be ready for it anytime. Those who avoid discussions on death topic are the ones who are afraid of it the most.
- One must understand that death is an opportunity to meet God and get liberation. We must accept death with dignity, not just for our death but for everyone around us.
- All of our relationships/relatives will die either before or after us. Nothing is permanent so why fear or worry about losing anything. You don't own it permanently either so why suffocate yourself if you have something (materialistic) or do not have it?
- Death is a very painful experience. It is a separation of body and soul. We can reduce the pain of death with the power of our thoughts. If we channel our thoughts toward God during death, the pain becomes bearable and we get relived faster.

- The thought process that we carry during our entire life plays important role in deciding our thinking at the last stage of life. We must practice avoiding thinking of losing our relationship, wealth, close family, pain or fear etc during the last stage of life. These are the glue of attachment that binds us to the next birth and we are forced to take rebirth if we think about these.

- Like death, rebirth is also certain for many of us. It is not a good thing as our pain gets multi-fold in the next life and suffering grows so we must pray for liberation or Mukti i.e., freedom from the cycle of birth and rebirth

- The method is very simple, one must remember and pray to God and request him to accept you as is by forgiving your sins. And in all probability, we may get liberation. However, you must pray to God at the last minute of your breadth which is the most difficult part.

- We must devote ourselves to God. Our belief systems and the thought process can change at different stages of life. Spirituality is real knowledge and the sooner we get it, is better for us.

- Spirituality makes us strong. Spirituality teaches us the real meaning of life, and how to make it enriching. Religion and faith could vary in people but the teachings across religions are to serve others and devotion to God.

- We may not get what we desire during this life, so God gives us one more chance to fulfill our pending desire in form of new life (after our death).

- If people are given an option to get birth in the next life in the same form, the majority of us would pick it. This is our ignorance that we pick rebirth instead of liberation. We can sense the problems with our thought processes easily. It needs self-inspection.

- It's our inability and ignorance that we often chose the wrong things during life and also during the end of our life. And our pain continues during this life as well as in the next life too.

- Check it yourself: Are you attached to relations, money, wealth or positions, or are you ready to leave it anytime any day, and devote yourself to God. Very few amongst us would have such courage. And only people with spiritual acumen would accept it openly.

- Our life is a reflection of our thinking and the choices we make. We must make careful choices in life. Let's make us immune so that we get spiritual and ready to give up this life to God and make death a peaceful experience to attain liberation, the one unique opportunity to meet God.

CHAPTER X

The Divine Knowledge: Connecting the Dots

Creation is a manifestation of God. The entire world, galaxies, multiple universes, every creature, life, etc all are created by God. He is the supreme power who creates, manages and destroys everything from time to time. He is the one who witnesses every life across universes, however, he is not influenced nor attached to anything. He is present everywhere; every soul is run by his energy but he himself is not affected by anything. God is everywhere outside us as well as within us (in our hearts) as per Bhagavad Gita.

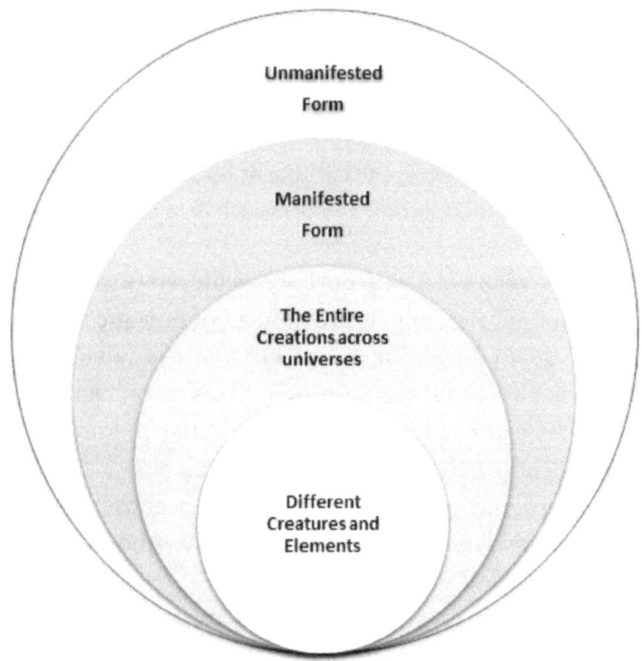

Where can we find God?

People often get confused about if God has a unique personality or a form. Few assume that God has taken birth(s) in different avatars so he must be having a father or a mother. Our mind often thinks within the physical dimensions and their boundaries and we hardly understand the spiritual dimensions. **God is unborn, eternal, immoral, latent and exists in unmanifested form.** He however can take any form to reflect on his manifested form which we can relate to easily. Our intellect and imagination are not yet matured enough to appreciate the unmanifested form (which you can relate to complete darkness), so we often relate everything with some shapes or form to visualize the presence. In the Hindu religion, people worship many Gods and Goddesses. But in reality, as per Bhagavad Gita, there is only one supreme power who has created millions of different Gods and Goddesses. These God and Goddesses are the manifestations of various powers of the Almighty. The Almighty has given each of us the freedom to worship anyone as per our choices and belief. God and Goddesses are the creation of the Almighty. In end, there is only one superpower which is the Almighty.

A simple way to relate the multiple avatars of God and Goddesses is to think of an organization with various departments many different kinds of people exist and each of them performs their duties and roles. Each individual is given an authority threshold to exercise his or her power. Gods and Goddesses get their power from the Supreme Almighty. They have been assigned different departments to run by the Almighty and are given different powers. They also have the liberty to give away some part of their powers to others (human beings) as awards or blessings. And they offer us their blessings as per their powers within some limits. And our prayers ultimately go to the Almighty directly or indirectly based on whom we pray. For running the world and different universes, there is a clear division of work amongst the God and Goddesses. This is similar to delegation and empowerment that we too follow.

Those who do not believe in God or any such form (Atheist) will never attain God and they never get liberation. This is mentioned in Bhagavad Gita. Such people are ignorant and are forced to take numerous birth and rebirth in the endless cycle of life. Every creature of the world resides or dwells within the lord supreme however he does not dwell in them. The soul is just a minuscule portion of his energy and we must realize that a portion in itself is not the whole object. The mighty wind is present and free to move everywhere however it rests always in the sky, likewise, all living beings always rest in the almighty. There is no existence of creatures without God. We all indirectly live within the Almighty. He is holding all of us. Like the wind cannot exist independently without the sky, similarly, the soul has no independent existence without God.

Under the direction of God, the material energy (Prakriti) produces all living and non-living forms of creatures and elements. And because of the material energy power (Prakriti), the changes happen in this world (creation, maintenance, and ending of the world). And that is the reason, no one can recognize God even when he takes form as a human to give a divine message to the world due to our ignorance. We are not capable of recognizing the Almighty. The Maya of God creates such an illusion that makes him unrecognizable or we doubt his presence and existence. However, some great pure souls can recognize and experience God as the origin of this universe and those are the ones who devote themselves to believing in God without any questions. Such devotees are always surrendering themselves to God and worshiping him all the time during their entire life.

The almighty is everything. He is the Vedic ritual, the sacrifice, the herbs and the Vedic mantra. He is the father, mother, and grandfather of the universe. He is the purifier, the goal of knowledge and the sacred syllable Om (Aum). He is the Rig Veda, Sam Veda and Yajurveda. God must be the supreme goal of life for everyone. He is the master, witness, abode, shelter and friend. He is the origin, end and resting place of creation. God radiates heat as the sun as well as send rain. He is immortal as well as the death personified. He is the spirit as well as the matter. Everything that you can think or imagine, is either God or his divine power.

Based on our beliefs and faith, we practice our religion. Those who worship God, are born amongst God and those who pray their ancestors are born amongst them and those who worship ghosts take birth amongst such beings, however, almighty's devotees always come to him i.e., they go to the param Dham. There is a rebirth of everyone including that of Gods and Goddesses (excluding the Almighty, the supreme God). By dedicating all our work to the almighty, we are freed from the bondage of good or bad results. Almighty treats everyone with the same love and affection and with the same parity. He is neither hostile nor partial to anyone. Even if we devote simple flowers, fruits, a leaf or even water to him, he will accept it with love. Almighty does not need anything from us. He loves our devotion. We must devote our everything to him.

Even if the sinner worship with full devotion, the Almighty treats them as saint and righteous as such individual has made the resolve to accept and surrender to God. The devotee of God will never be lost or destroyed and ultimately gains lasting peace and reach liberation once a step is made towards devotion. We all must devote ourselves to the almighty, worship him and offer obeisance towards him. One must always think of God, devote themselves, worship him and once your mind and body are dedicated towards the Almighty, you certainly will attain him.

Here is a learning and quick reference for this chapter: -

- There are misconceptions amongst people who think Bhagavad Gita teaches us to leave everything and become a sadhu or a monk. This is completely wrong. People often get confused here and read devotion as a substitute for giving up duties and responsibilities
- Bhagavad Gita indicates focusing on duties, the Karmayog is the foundation of the Gita. The importance of Karma, the power of intelligence and choosing the right karma (chapters 3,4 and 5) are the progressing steps in the Gita that we must follow to attain next level of knowledge.
- Karmayog teaches us to do right duties, duties without attachments and use our intellect (not emotions) to make decisions, at the same time isolating ourselves from the outcome (success or failure)
- The Karmayog (learnings of right duties) and Gyanyog (using our mind and intellect intelligently for making decisions) are the initial steps towards becoming a stronger individual who can differentiate between right and wrong in life and can pick right karma (duties) and face any circumstances
- Every chapter in Gita is a step toward attaining the next level of intelligence. The Bhaktiyog (surrender) is the elevated state of devotion (and you must take steps of Karmayog and Gyanyog to reach Bhaktiyog) which is also called surrender to God. There are no shortcuts here
- Duties or Karmayog are the necessity for humans to survive so one cannot climb the ladder of Bhaktiyog without doing the duties of life.
- This chapter helps to understand God, its forms and his supreme qualities. God is formless as well exists in various forms which are his different manifestations. He is eternal, immoral, latent and exists in unmanifested form too. He exists as soul energy within us and as divine energy everywhere.
- Almighty is the creator, savior and destructor of this world and every creature across universes.

- He is one and the only supreme power that ever existed, He plays a witness role without indulging in anything. God is just to everyone. It is our karma that decides our life and afterlife, including the cycle of birth and rebirth and liberation
- We have to make the right choices in life. We have complete freedom here and Gita guides us to pick what is important for each of us and how to get there but does not force anything on us
- With the right knowledge, one can easily realize and understand that there is nothing more important, caring and powerful than the Almighty and one must devote themselves to the Almighty
- With devotion, we can free ourselves from the endless cycle of birth and rebirth and pain and can attain liberation by doing just duties without any expectation, attachments and fear.
- The divine knowledge teaches us the importance of devotion, power of God and understanding of God with its other qualities
- The devotee of God will never be lost or destroyed and ultimately gains lasting peace and reach liberation. Even if one does not get liberation in this life, one can always make attempts to become a good human being

CHAPTER XI

Decoding the power of Almighty

Almighty is the origin and primary source of everything. We may refer to it by a different name but we all know and broadly accept that there is some superpower that is running everything under the universe. This is a standard belief across humankind. We have seen in the previous chapter about the Almighty being present in the manifested and unmanifested form. Every creation, every element that one can think of is created and powered by the Almighty. (If you believe in superpower theory, then you should not question the presence of a superpower everywhere, and every power belonging or surrendering to him). The different God, Goddesses, saints and every creature across the universes are created by the Almighty.

Our belief system evolves based on experience and trust. Spirituality is also experiential learning that one can feel within, around and experience personally. Those who believe in God, do not question his powers nor care about what others say about God. This chapter is more about understanding the power of God as articulated by Lord Krishna in the Bhagavad Gita.

Almighty is the one who created all the universes, living and non-living elements within in. God and Goddesses (as prayed in the Hindu religion) are created as well after the formation of the earth and other planets by the Almighty. The one who ever existed in unborn form is the Almighty. He is the one who created everything. Everything is his manifestation. Only the Almighty has the supreme knowledge, supreme power and supreme existence. Rest all is temporary across universes.

As a human, our intellect forces us to challenge everything. Sometimes we do it for curiosity, some time to learn new things and the majority of the time to prove our points or knowledge (due to ego). **Our thoughts, emotions and belief system either transform us or make us perish.** Those who have trust and believe in the Almighty, will never question its existence, power and kindness as such people are clear in their minds and clear in thinking. After facing the ups and downs in life and learning from it, such people (who we call devotees) have developed a level of trust which no one can alter. The person who considers the Almighty ahead of everything is the true devotee. Such people are free from attachments and enjoy life peacefully (not as a burden nor as guilt but rather as a gift of God to serve

God and others). But for others, it is not easy to blindly believe God. We are still witnessing life and are confused. We are neither true devotees nor atheists. We are still deciding and questioning is it true? And by the time we get to understand more, we are already dead. And many times, it is too late to experience the divinity and often, we are forced to take multiple births and go through lots of pain (mental, physical and emotional) to get to that level of understanding, to upgrade our spiritual knowledge. This all is fair and is part of the broader play of God.

All the qualities of humans (good or bad) are derived from the Almighty. He has created all the good and evil around us and given us choices to pick the things as per our preferences and knowledge level. We all have freedom of choice. God never forces us to get attracted towards attachment, neither does he gives us pain and problems (pains are due to non-fulfilment of our desires). God gives us different situations; he gives us qualities, knowledge and environment to deal with those. It is mostly our greed and expectations that make us face pain, grief, anger, fear and attachments.

People who understand life from a spiritual lens are inclined toward developing divine qualities such as forgiveness, self-satisfaction, truth, controlling emotions, clarity in thoughts, clear purpose and the ability to manage extreme situations in life. And such people by in large are not God-fearing but God-loving people who are either on the spiritual path or want to get there. You can relate the qualities of people to a powerhouse/ electrical grid that is used differently in different gadgets and produces different effects. It may create sound in one, light in other and heat in the third. You can relate it to the different behavior of people around you. All these individuals carry the same soul energy within us that is derived from God but their actions are different. People use their energy for different things This is a simple example to relate to why each of us is different and behaves differently.

We need to exercise control and use our soul energy for a meaningful purpose. Otherwise, we are wasting our lives on this planet. Running away for life or running around with materialistic objects/ possessions/ belongings cannot be the sole purpose of this life. If the soul is beautiful, we need to make our life beautiful too. This is our duty and responsibility too.

Those who devote themselves to God get the blessings of God. They get clarity in life, get a clear purpose and God helps them enrich their life. Without devotion, one cannot attain peace. Our attachments, arrogance, ego, etc are driven due to the influence of Rajoguna and Tamoguna on us.

The pure Satvaguna makes us pure and helps develop divine qualities. With God's blessing, we develop Satvaguna, so that the Maya (the illusionary power of God), does not influence us and we are not impacted by the distractions in life. Trust and devotion to God is the only way to experience and enjoy such a state. And such people who are on the path of devotion are well-taken care of by God himself. They are never destroyed nor perish.

On request on Arjuna, Krishna explains his different forms and power. While Arjuna does not doubt the capabilities, power and supremacy of Krishna, he is curious to learn more and get his ignorance cleared. The almighty is the soul energy that resides in our hearts. He is the beginning, middle and end of every creature in the universe. Let's understand the power of God as expressed in Bhagavad Gita per the below table. It indicates that every source of energy and creation is within God.

- ✓ Amongst the twelve sons of Aditi, he is the Vishnu
- ✓ Amongst the luminous objects, he is the sun
- ✓ Amongst the start, he is the moon
- ✓ Amongst the Vedas, he is the Samaveda (the musical song for praising God)
- ✓ Amongst the celestial Gods, he is Indra
- ✓ Amongst the senses, he is the mind
- ✓ Amongst the living beings, he is the consciousness
- ✓ Amongst the 11 Rudra, he is Shankar
- ✓ Amongst the 8 vasus, he is Agni (fire). The 8 vasus are (land, water, fire, air, space, sun, moon and stars)
- ✓ Amongst purifiers, he is the wind
- ✓ Amongst wielders of weapons, he is Lord Rama.
- ✓ Amongst water creatures, he is the crocodile
- ✓ Amongst flowing rivers, he is the Ganges.
- ✓ He is the all-devouring death and the origin of those things that are yet to be born
- ✓ Amongst the descendants of Vrishini (dynasty), he is Krishna
- ✓ Amongst the Pandavas, he is Arjun
- ✓ Amongst the sages, he is the Ved Vyas

- ✓ Amongst the seers/sages, he is the Bhrigu (Lord Vishnu holds the mark of his feet on his chest when Bhrigu was testing the patience level of trinity of Brahma, Vishnu and Shiv)
- ✓ Amongst different sounds, he is Om(Aum) sound Amongst the snakes, he is Anant
- ✓ Amongst aquatics, he is Varun
- ✓ Amongst dispensers of law, he is Yamraj, the king of death.
- ✓ Amongst the departed ancestors, he is Aryama (3rd son of Aditi, as head of ancestors)
- ✓ Amongst the mountains, he is Meru (a golden mountain that stands in centre of universe and axis of the world)
- ✓ Amongst the great thinkers, he is Sukracharya
- ✓ Amongst secrets, he is the silence
- ✓ Amongst the wise, he is their wisdom
- ✓ Amongst feminine qualities, he is the fame, prosperity, fine speech, memory, intelligence, courage and forgiveness.
- ✓ In short, everything that is perfect reflects the manifestation of the Almighty and his energy
- ✓ He is "just" punishment amongst means of preventing lawlessness
- ✓ He is the generating seed of all living beings

Decoding the power of God

This is a short list. With such knowledge and understanding, there should not be any need for learning any new form of knowledge about God. Simply know that with one fraction of Almighty, God pervades/encompass and supports the entire creation.

Here is a learning and quick reference for this chapter: -

- God is the source of every creation, every quality, attribute and every aspect which we can imagine

- We exist because of him and he is present in form of soul energy within each of us. We should be thankful to God for giving us such closeness and his blessings
- We own nothing, really nothing. Everything belongs to him. Till we hold our ego and ignorance, we will never trust and believe in God
- Surrender, devotion and trust in God are the basic tenets to get his blessings. He would take care of us and we need not worry about anything.
- The difference between good, bad, ugly, etc will get clearer once we start our spiritual journey and God guides us to pick the right thing in our life from time to time.
- We have been given intelligence by God. However, as a human, we can never pick the bests things for us due to the limitations of our minds. Spirituality teaches a method to connect with God and learn about his teachings and lessons which are written in Vedic scriptures
- The guidance can be obtained through a teacher or by God himself. And when everything is being created by God, controlled by God, it is in our best interest to get guidance (read as blessings) from God. Spirituality decodes that knowledge.
- God is the supreme power that powers the universes and every creature underneath it. We need to imbibe good qualities that elevate our level as a human and gives meaning to this life.
- We will be leaving this life someday sooner or later; we should leave this world with satisfaction and peace by doing something meaningful in life (which is not self-driven). Spirituality can help here.
- The extreme state of knowledge is divine knowledge. With the help of God (and with assistance from a teacher) we can learn it.
- It is in our best interest to become better human beings, better individuals personally, professionally, sociality and spiritually.
- We need to tune our thoughts and our belief system and need practice to adopt the Bhagavad Geeta learnings in our day-to-day life. It is difficult but not impossible.

CHAPTER XII

Experiencing the Divine form of God

Many of us believe in God, and carry an image in our minds of God. In most likelihood, this image represents the great superpower who is kind, beautiful and caring. The most extreme form of greatness can be related to God. Arjuna was also curious and keen to witness God, his shape, color and other characteristics, so he requested Krishna to show him his divine form. This is also referred to as Vishwarupa Darshan in Bhagavad Gita.

As an individual, we are not capable of viewing God and his form. The reason is we are born as the physical body (material) whereas God is spiritual. Our eyes are not capable of viewing God. We need divine eyes to experience him. So many of us can still feel God based on our imagination power. It does not matter what your mind shows you, what matters the most is your faith, belief and devotion. We must respect the faith and belief of everyone when it comes to God.

Vishwarupa - The gigantic form of God

We need purity and peace of mind to even visualize God. The images, symbols, statues, etc that we trust and pray for are a reflection of our belief systems on God and this must be respected by all religions. Only with God's blessings and his wish, we can experience him as a whole. You may refer to him as a manifested form or unmanifested form, both are representing God, the superpower. God decides who is pure enough to experience him and get his blessings.

God is the creator of every universe; he is the possessor of every creature across universes. He is the source of energy for every planet, galaxies, human soul and anything one can visualize. When Arjuna sees God in front of him, he experiences the infinite form comprising all the universes. Arjuna witnessed the entire creation in the body of God, he sees the

Almighty with unlimited arms, unlimited faces and stomachs. There is no beginning or end and his form extends immeasurably in all directions. His radiance is similar to a thousand suns blazing together in the sky. Krishna shows the twelve Aditya, eight vasus, eleven Rudra, two Ashwini kumaras as well as the forty-nine Maruts within himself.

Arjuna experiences all other Gods, saints, Brahma, Shiva, and every God within the Almighty. He sees the many mouths bearing terrible teeth, resembling the raging fires in front of him. All the creatures are entering the mouth of Almighty and Arjuna sees their heads smash between the terrible teeth of the God. Arjuna is terrified and asks for the reason for such a dangerous shape and form and the purpose of the existence of the Almighty.

Krishna tells him: I am the mighty time, the source of destruction that comes forth to annihilate/ destroy the world. He tells him that everyone, all warriors are already been killed by him or will get killed by him, so he just needs to obey his duty (as per the wish of the lord mighty) to establish the dharma (justice i.e., the righteous thing) in this world. Arjuna is not able to tolerate or face the radiance and extremely dangerous appearance of the Almighty and requests for forgiveness of all his sins and mistakes that he had committed in life. He requests Krishna to show him his softer form which he is used to seeing. At his request, Krishan comes back to his normal form. He first shows him his Narayan form (the divine form with 4 hands) and later comes back to the human form.

Arjuna now realizes his mistake of questioning and requesting proof of existence from God. He realizes that everything belongs to the Almighty, the reason for everything is the Almighty and the reason for all births and destructions is the Almighty. Krishan tells him that no one can ever experience such form. Only the pure devotee like him gets a chance in a lifetime to view or experience such a divine form of God.

We all are too tiny; our existence is like a bubble in this world. Our pride and ego give us an illusion of our big status in society. We are nothing. Once we realize it, our ego can settle down and we can at least make an attempt to live a better human life, a spiritual life that does not mean just doing prayers, but doing our duties without harming anyone and being thankful to God for everything. We must thank and express our gratitude in a spiritual world. It is the union /Yog with God to attain or at least develop some fraction of the qualities of God so that we purify ourselves.

Almighty is a creator as well as the destroyer. We are already been created (born), so we must be ready for our destruction (death). Almighty owns everything. We have no right to question him. He knows everything and he knows what is best for us. We should not waste our life in the intellectual struggle to find what is the purpose of our life and where we will be heading. We all are heading towards our death which is the reality of life. You may imagine God in softer form, in extreme form or as a formless God. It does not matter. Everything belongs to the Almighty and we must surrender it to him. Almighty will anyways take it back someday. He does not need anything from us.

He has created everything. For him, it is a play to teach a lesson to people who distract themselves from the spiritual path. Almighty is everywhere, in every creature including different God and Goddesses whom we pray to. We should thank him for his amazing creations and wonders. In end, we must try to unite with him. (Even if we do not want, someday we will unite him after our numerous births once we get purity). Spirituality is about union with God. It teaches us the good deeds in life. It teaches us to attain divinity by treating everyone as a portion of God. The is the basis of spirituality to attain purification of self.

Here is a learning and quick reference for this chapter: -

- We can experience the divine form of God with purity in heart and with devotion.
- We should never question why others pray in a specific form or shape of God. It is the belief of individuals, and we must respect it. As long as someone is not causing you harm or harm to society, we should give everyone respect and space for their belief
- We have choices to visualize, imagine and pray to any form of God. The world is divided on the topic of God, types of Gods, power of God, your God, my God and many such divisions. God is just one. Size, shape and form do not matter as those are the boundaries we have given to God.
- Spirituality is about union with God, our union and purification with God to treat everyone similarly to serve society without any harm to anyone. We must build our own yardstick to first judge ourselves and then compare others. Without self-purity, we should not become advisors for others.
- We all have a short stay or temporary life in this world, so we must utilize it in a positive way and develop qualities that we expect in others most of the time. We expect love, kindness and respect from others but never assess how poor are we within us when it comes to these qualities.

Please do your self-assessment before preaching to others

- God exists in forms that we can relate to with ease. For a spiritual experience of God, we need spiritual dimensions and learning.
- God is a source of every energy, the positive energy that exists everywhere
- When our mind is inclined towards devotion and prayers, we feel positive energy or positive vibrations. That reflects the existence of God's energy around us. Very few of us can feel it.
- God is not just a feeling; it is the reason for our existence. We must make our lives meaningful so that we can use the positive energy for some good deeds to help others.
- If we can feel the positive vibrations of God, And with God's blessings there is a possibility that we may experience divine energy someday in our life. All it needs is devotion and trust. Spirituality helps you unite with God. It is a path towards divinity.
- We must make attempts for spiritual union with God. This develops purity in mind and actions. Spirituality should be the end of our life. Those who realize it early, start their spiritual journey ahead. For others, it is never too late to start spirituality.

CHAPTER XIII

Understanding devotion: Find qualities that God loves

We all have different beliefs and follow different worship styles. Few of us believe that the Almighty does not have a shape i.e., nirakaar or formless while others believe that there are different shapes and forms that exist of the Almighty. Arjuna tries to ask Krishna who is supreme here: Is the individual who worships a shapeless God? or the one who prays the shaped form of the God!

As per Krishna, it does not matter. As long as someone fixes their mind on God and always engages in devotion with strong faith, the individual is considered the best yogi. The objective of both types of believers is to attain God so they are involved in their best practices to attain God. The devotion matters, the rest is secondary. The individuals who are engaged in the devotion and welfare of every human being, attain God.

Those who believe and pray to God in its shapeless form are equally important however such a path is difficult and painful because for ages humans have lived and experienced the physical form, our daily conducts are with physical forms (other humans and objects in this world) so aligning ourselves and our mental mind to a formless God is a difficult journey. Those who can relate themselves beyond the physical body, find it easy to align to the formless avatar of God. The worship of God in a formless form is more difficult than its formed appearance.

One must fix his or her mind on God and surrender your intellect to God, thereupon you will always live in God. In case you are not able to focus your mind and intellect on God, you must practice and develop a strong desire to attain God (in form of getting rid of impurities or bad traits). Human purification is possible only with this method. Once your senses get holy with prayers of God and actions for God, you are directly in connection with God.

In case you are not able to fully focus on God or develop a desire to attain God, you need to devote your karma or actions to perform devotional services for God, thereby you will achieve a state of perfection or completeness. Even if you are not able to perform devotional service, then one must do his regular duties but should become detached from the fruits of your actions. There are many options available to us that can give us inner peace. We need to train our mind and convince it of things which we either ignore or find difficult to accept.

Knowledge is superior to our mechanical practices. Meditation or focus is superior to knowledge and becoming detached from the outcome or results is far better than meditation. This gives us the ultimate peace within ourselves.

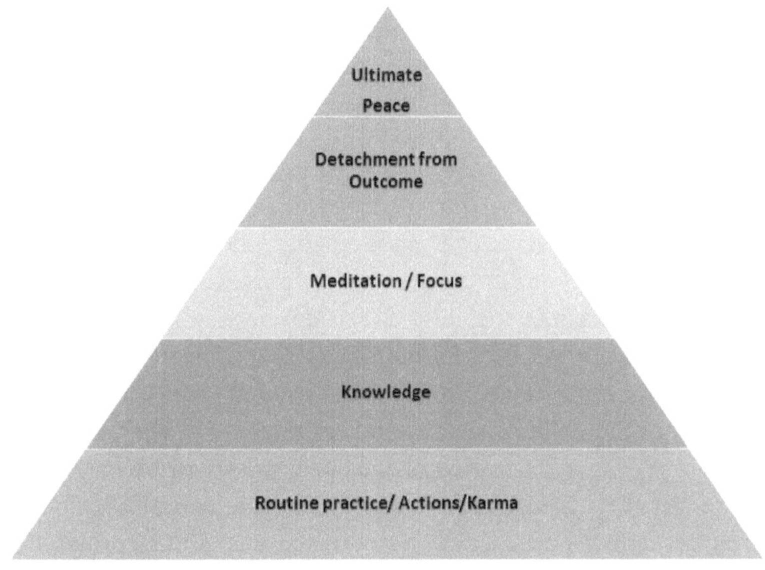

Path to Divinity

We often complain about God not supporting or favoring us or our actions. A few calls God even cruel and insensitive to human feelings. God does not accept us because we are impure due to our various bad qualities ranging from ego, anger, greed, desires, expectations and fear. God cannot accept impurities. We can attain God only when we are pure within. We will get his unconditional love once we surrender to him with complete devotion. It requires trust and belief in God. We often look at God with self-doubts, we try to assess the existence of God and many such things due to our ignorance. With such a broken level of trust, we can never attain God. We look towards God when we either face challenges and pain or when we desire something from life. We have made God a topic of our convenience.

And that is the reason, we do not feel his presence as devotion is missing in many of us. Spirituality is union with God. With impurities and lack of devotion and trust, we cannot get God or his blessings. God expects us to be pure (purity of mind, soul and thoughts).

God is very kind. Everything is happening in this world at the wish of God, we are just participating and he is observing our actions closely. We are sent into this world with the purpose to purify ourselves. The cycle of birth and death is an endless loop that will not finish till we get pure and possess divine qualities within ourselves. Devotion is unconditional love. We must ask ourselves are we loving God unconditionally or do we love him so that he can fulfill our desires? We are selfish so we do not get his attention and love.

To get God's love and attention, one must be selfless, free from malice toward all living beings, friendly and kind to everyone, one must be free from arrogance and ego. One must be free from attachments to possessions and should treat happiness and distress equally (should not be impacted by the good or bad situation in life), one must possess forgiveness qualities, one must be determined, satisfied and happy in any situation, one must devote to God. Such qualities make a person pure. Such devotees are the ones whom God really loves. Now you must assess and compare yourself and ask how many of such qualities you really possess. These are the basic qualification one must possess to get true love and attention from God.

This is not the exhaustive list of qualities of a true devotee. One who does not get provoked or never become reasons of any provocation to anytime, one who is equal in pleasure and pain and free from fear and anxieties, such devotee is dear to God. One who is indifferent to gain, not fearful or does not need anyone's support (apart from God), externally and internally pure, skilful, free from self-interest, and does not expect anything in return from anyone and true devotee of God is very dear to the God.

One who does not get impacted by pleasure neither despair in sorrow or grief, one who does not desire anything, one who has given up or isolated himself from thinking of good or bad, one who is full of devotion is very dear to the God.

This is not the end of qualities that one must possess to get attention and love of God. The list of divine qualities is really long and it help us realize that we are too bad or impure to reach the state of purity that a true devotee must possess. One must also be neutral to friends and foes, one must treat the appreciation and insults in similar way of neutrality, one must be same in situation of gain or loss, one must be away from poor friendship or relationship (bad people), one must be neutral during criticism or appreciation by anyone, one must be satisfied in any situation, one must be attachment free (free from attachment or affection of loved or dear ones), one must be intelligent, firm believer and a true devotee. Such people are very dear to the God.

Those who make God their ultimate objective, believe and devote themselves to God, and follow the divine knowledge shared by God are the ones whom God loves the most.

Here is a learning and quick reference for this chapter: -

- Our belief systems may be different but the God is one. It does not matter if we pray the formless or any form of God. The objective of every religion is devotion and service to God.
- As long as someone fixes their mind on God and always engages in devotion with strong faith and good karma, one can get God's blessings but this is not easy. Devotion is unconditional love to God (having no expectations in return)
- One must develop qualities that are loved by God. Purity of soul, humanity, respect and care for everyone is one of the basic qualities one must possess
- Attaining God is not an easy path. It demands us to think beyond self, beyond our relationship and religion, beyond liking or disliking, becoming situation agnostic, free from attachments, ego, desires, indifferent to different things such as gain or loss, respect or insult, appreciation or criticism are some basic qualities we must develop to get the attention of God
- We must develop qualities to get purity in every aspect of life and it requires practice, devotion, belief and determination
- Spirituality helps us make our belief system stronger and develop the qualities of a good human being. Devotion is the only way to attain God and the path to devotion is not easy.

CHAPTER XIV

Understanding our body and soul

In spirituality, people talk about body and soul. We have been told that our body is temporary and our soul is eternal. This seems logical if we assume the soul as some form of energy. We all know that when a soul leaves, we are just a dead body. This indicates that our body is different than our soul. Now the question is: are you a body or a soul or both? What is the relationship between the body and the soul? If the soul resides within the body, then isn't the body superior to the soul? Let's understand some of these aspects. Our body is our karma field i.e., the area that enables us to perform various activities or karma whereas the soul is the one (power or energy) that governs, runs and empowers the body. This makes the soul as superior to our body. The soul contains all the qualities of God and it is a fraction of God. Soul is divine.

In Bhagavad Gita, the body is referred to as **Kshetra** (the area or perimeter or field that performs activities) and the soul is referred to as **kshetragya** (the one who knows the area or the field very well). The soul is also called Atma whereas the lord supreme is called Parmatma, the one who knows every soul across universes. If we refer to a soul as a type of energy, thus the body is nothing but the field of the energy. If you consider the soul magnetic or kinetic energy, then any motion in our body is nothing but our actions or movements of body parts (body) itself. The person who can relate to and differentiate the body, soul and the Almighty, holds true knowledge.

We understood a bit so far about the soul but how about the body? Our body is made up of 24 elements (from a spiritual lens). The soul does not change but our bodies change continuously. We all have witnessed changes in our body all the time. Our good, bad or ugly behavior is because of the influence or changes happening on our body (which includes the mind).

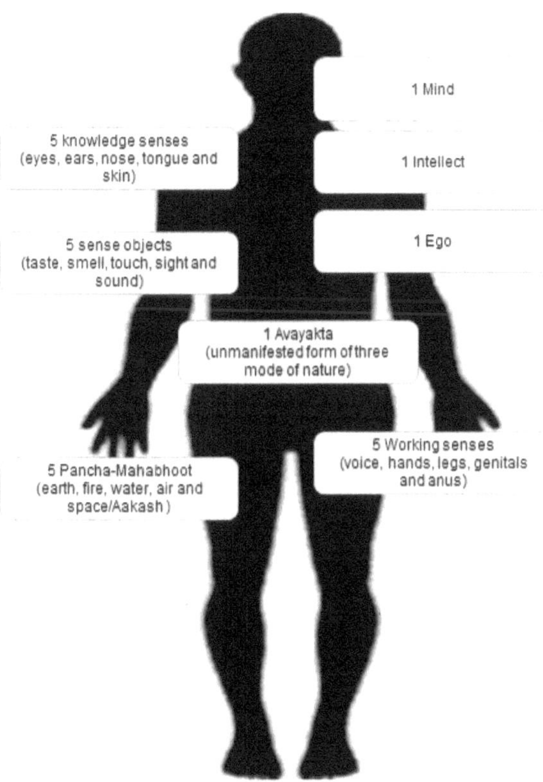

24 Elements of our body

The 24 elements of the human body include Pancha-mahabhoot (5) that includes the **earth, fire, water, air and space/Aakash** + our Intellect (1) + Ego (1) + Avayakta (1) (an unmanifested form of three modes of nature) + our **knowledge senses** (5) that contain our eyes, ears, nose, tongue and skin + working **senses** (5) that includes voice, hands, legs, genitals and anus) + 5 **sense objects** (taste, smell, touch, sight and sound) + our **mind** (1)

The desire-hate, happiness-misery, consciousness and determination is the different interest area of the body that pulls us to do different activities. The good or bad is based on what we desire and how our body acts towards those subjects. Each element of the body has its own characteristics. *Our intellect, mind and ego (which are 3 different elements of our body) need to be in control* for becoming good human being. Our body supports the soul in its quest for happiness in the world, as the soul guides it continuously.

What is knowledge and what is ignorance? Lord Krishna makes a clear distinction here. Humbleness, freedom from hypocrisy, Non-violence, Forgiveness, Simplicity, Service of Guru, cleanliness of body and mind, persistent/determination, self-control, dispassion/detachment towards objects of senses, absence of ego, awareness towards the reality of birth, aging, disease and death cycle, non-attachment, absence of clinging/ attraction to the spouse, children, home and related stuff, even-mindedness towards desired and undesired events in life, constant and exclusive devotion of the Almighty, the inclination for solitary/lonely places, aversion of mundane society, constancy in spiritual knowledge and pursuit of the absolute truth. All these are part of true knowledge as per Krishna. **Anything outside this is pure ignorance.**

God encompasses everything around us, including within each of us. God has his hands, feet, eyes, head and faces everywhere across universes. Though his senses are covering everything, he does not have any physical senses (rather has spiritual senses). This may seem contrary but in a spiritual sense, God is a master and cluster of numerous contradictory qualities. God is around us; he is within us as well. He is too far from us at the same time very near to us. God is the source of light in all luminaries. He is knowledge, the object of knowledge and the goal of knowledge. He dwells within the heart of all living beings as well. Our physical mind and intellect are not capable of understanding God because he is spiritual and our mind cannot think beyond physical boundaries.

In Bhagavad Gita, there are references to **Prakriti, Jeev, Purush and Param Purush.** It is important to understand what are those and how they are interlinked. Prakriti is nothing but the Maya (the primordial form of material energy). It has ever existed and originated from the Almighty. Many of us refer to it as the material nature or the material energy. She is the energy of God, so it has eternal existence. Our body itself is made up of a minuscule portion of the unmanifested form of 3 modes of Prakriti (refer to the 24 elements of the body in this chapter). And our body has direct influence by the Prakriti. Prakriti has 3 qualities i.e., Satva, Rajo and Tamo guna and our body gets pulled towards those Gunas.

Prakriti= Maya = Material energy = Energy of God

Jeev = Soul= Purush = Consciousness

Param Purush = Almight= Supreme God

Understanding Prakiriti, Soul and Almighty

We have the influence of these Guna/Maya on us all the time. Every human has the influence of these 3 guns of Prakriti on them. We seek to enjoy the material energy (Prakriti and its belongings).

Mother nature will keep attracting you towards itself (Maya) and its physical belongings (creations). You may assume Prakriti as a bigger magnet that attracts the smaller magnetic elements (our body) towards it and its possessions. There is a forceful pull and it is up to us which quality of Prakriti we want to get attracted to and which guna we want to dominate us. The Jeev is also known as Jeeva shakti which is nothing but our soul or soul energy. The Purush is another name for the individual soul. The soul energy is another pure energy of God that has ever existed. The Param Purush is the lord supreme.

Jeev/Soul and Prakriti are eternal. Both are the manifestation of God's energy. The soul is the living or conscious form whereas Prakriti is the material form of energy. God had given complete freedom to both the energies (soul and Prakriti) to govern and live. Both energies have been present ever since before the formation of the universes. **Every formation is due to the union of the Prakriti and soul (one of physical matter, the other is consciousness).** The soul is a portion of God's conscious energy that exists in every living being whereas Prakriti or Maya is the divine material energy of God that also has some presence in our body.

The power of Prakriti (Maya) is more powerful than soul energy (this is how God has designed it and empowered it). Maya controls every creature/ element within itself. In chapter 7, Krishna clearly says that it is very difficult to overcome the power of Maya. But those who surrender to God we can cross over it easily. The body (which has the same qualities as

Prakriti) gets attracted to the prakriti. Maya lures it.

Soul resides within the body to empower it with energy. Since the influence of Maya on the body (and indirectly on the soul) is extreme, we forget our duties towards God/soul energy and rather gets attracted towards the Maya or Prakriti and its belongings. Maya is sitting in between us and God. Those who understand it are clever. You have the choice to pick either Maya or God. Without spirituality, people make wrong choices in their life. Spirituality helps to understand the difference. The illusion of Maya is so high that we get distracted from our spiritual path. The moment the devotion comes into play, Maya itself helps individuals to attain God with the amplification of satva guna within us. The Maya or the material nature is responsible for all the cause and effect in the world. The material takes different forms and different species are produced by Prakriti on this earth. It is believed that there are 8.4 million species that exists in different shapes and forms due to the material form of the Maya or Prakriti.

The soul gets a body (field of activity) according to its past karma, and it often identifies itself with the body, mind and intellect. The soul needs the body for expression through the body. Thus, it seeks the pleasure of the bodily senses. When the senses come in contact with the sense objects, the mind experiences the pleasure sensation. In this way, the body experiences the sensation of both pleasure and pain, through the medium of the senses, mind and intellect. The almighty is also present in our heart (In fact he is everywhere, internally and externally in minuscule as well as in large form, the spiritual form). The Almighty observes the soul and its activities.

Our soul keeps reminding the body to get rid of the dominance or attraction towards the Prakriti and its creations. But body ignorance as it has a higher influence of Maya (compared to sole). God observes the act of our body and soul continually and our next life is based on the karma of the body. We have learned earlier in chapter 2 that the soul changes bodies after death i.e., it moves from one body to another similar to a person changing cloths. Just as a person discards his old clothes and adorns new ones, the soul keeps changing bodies from one lifetime to another till it gets liberated.

The soul is the eternal energy; the energy of God and it must remain pure. However, when it comes in contact with the body (due to the influence of material elements), it loses its purpose (due to the presence of the ego element of the body) and gets attached to the worldly pleasures (which it experiences through the body, mind and intellect) either to enjoy or to dominate on the nature. It gets derailed. One of the main reasons for the soul identifying itself as the body is due to the influence of ego, ignorance and Maya which makes the soul forget its original purpose. The original purpose of the soul is to understand the body and guide it to perform divine activities. Recollect the Kshetra and Kshetragya definitions that we learned at the beginning of this chapter. Ideally, a Kshetragya should guide the body and provide divine wisdom or knowledge to the body. The soul gets punished indirectly for failing to guide the body. Our actions that we perform via our body can either distract us to seek worldly pleasures (attraction towards Prakriti) or towards the soul (for self-realization and attaining peace). We have choices to pick.

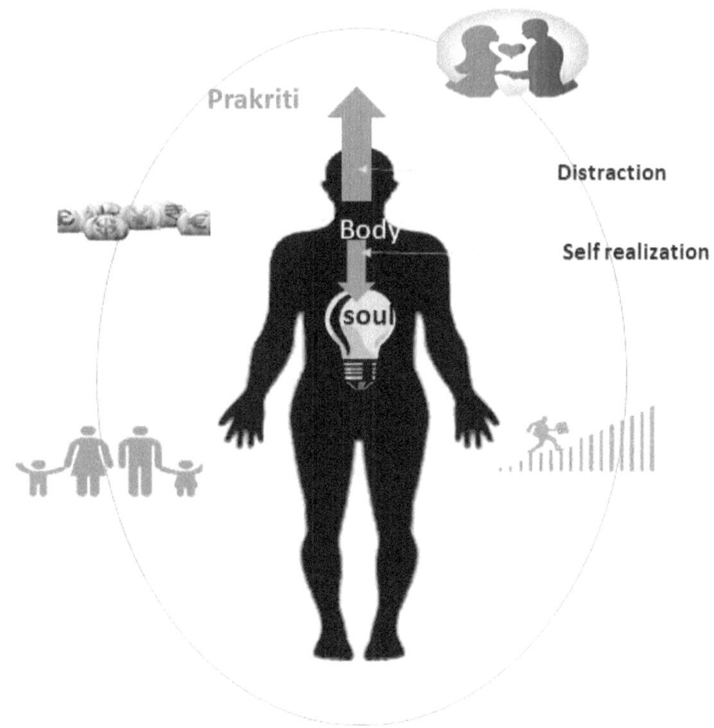

Understanding Self-realization and Distraction

When we as human gets attached to the Prakriti or its possessions (material gain), we move away from the spiritual path. It is the choice between the divine vs the material. Our intellect needs to work sensibly. The Parmatma is the observer of every activity of the body, soul and every human being. Since the body should be governed by the soul, the soul is being held responsible for every action of the body, good or bad. The soul gets the punishment to get purity in a new body. Soul needs to be pure for attaining liberation. Maya ensures that she continuously derails soul energy away from God through the body. The soul is held captive by the body that body gets pulled towards the Maya. Maya has been instructed by God to create an illusion so that people use their intellect to pick right and wrong. i.e., spiritual vs material in life. Everything in this universe happens and exists due to the union of consciousness soul and the material Prakriti. When the soul regains its purity, it gets liberated.

The body is temporary but the soul is eternal. The divine knowledge is to get rid of our impurities and develop devotion. We must understand the cycle of life, the influence of the soul and Prakriti, and the body and their interactions and side effects. Those who understand the truth about the supreme soul (the Almighty), the individual soul, material nature and the interaction of the three qualities of nature (satva, Rajo and Tamo), will not take birth here again. They will be liberated regardless of their present condition. Our body and karma are the main reason for our suffering. We need purity of body and our actions. This happens once we devote ourselves to God and spirituality. Those who can see God as the supreme soul that is present everywhere and in all living beings, do not degrade themselves by their mind and body.

They alone truly see the reality and understand that all actions (of the body) are performed by the material nature, while the embodied soul does nothing. The soul is God's energy. One must understand the influence of Body, Soul and Maya on us. The interplay between them is what we must understand.

The soul is different from the Body. Those who understand this, possess the real knowledge. The soul in reality does not get contaminated by the body (it has a divine nature). It is not affected by the body and its actions of it. Soul gives energy to the entire body to act. Bhagavad Gita guides us to purify our souls. When we associate ourselves as body (and not soul), we get trapped in the cycle of birth and rebirth. Since our body develops impurity and the soul being the master of it, gets the blame and punishment for the action of the body and is held responsible for punishment. Our desires force us to take a new birth into a new suitable body as per our karma, the soul too gets cascaded indirect punishment due to its failed attempt to purify ourselves.

Soul is captured within the body. And the body has the influence of Prakriti. Since mother nature is more powerful than the individual soul, the body gets tilted towards the possessions of worldly possessions (effect of Maya). The real objective of the soul is to guide our body. The body is made up of 5 sheaths/layers/Kosh in spirituality or in yoga. The soul resides within these layers. These are

- Aanmaya Kosh – The external layer of our body which we call the food body is made up of the Pancha mahabhoot i.e., the 5 gross elements (earth, water, fire, air and space). The primary driver of this Kosh is the food that we eat.

- Pranmaya Kosh- This layer resides insides the Anamaya Kosh and consists of 5 life airs (Pram, Apana, Vyan, Saman and Udan). The primary driver of this Kosh is the air we inhale and exhale

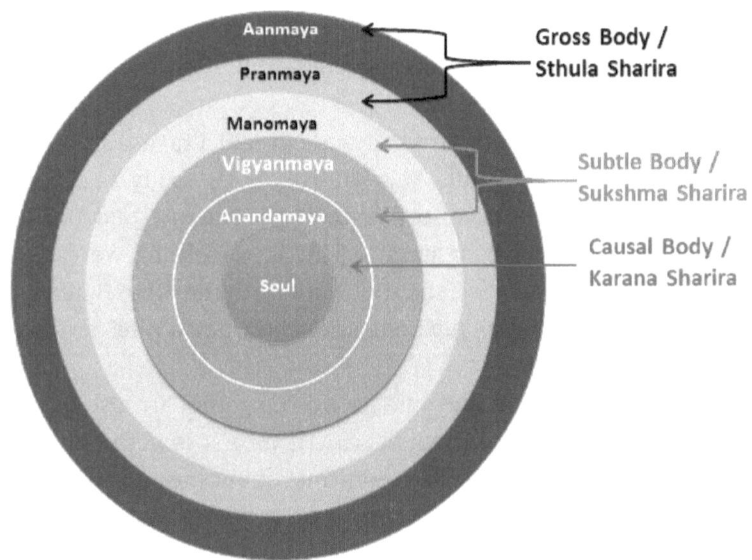

Different Kosh of Human Body

- Manomaya Kosh- This is the Mental sheet that is made up of the mind and 5 working senses (hands, legs, genitals, anus and voice). The primary driver of this Kosh is e our thoughts that originate from our working senses. Few refer to it as our sub-conscious mind too which governs our body without our conscience. (e.g., desire, urge). This Kosh makes the bondages with the world

- Vigyanmaya Kosh- This is the intelligence layer consisting of the intellect and the 5 knowledge senses (eyes, ear, tongue, nose and skin). The primary driver for this Kosh is that gives direction to our thoughts. Our perceptions and actions are driven by this Kosh. If our perceptions are wrong that creates an impurity in this Kosh.

- Aanandamaya Kosh – This is the innermost layer also called as bliss layer which consists of the ego. The primary driver for this Kosh is the happiness that comes within without any external cause. Since it is very near to the soul, it attracts the blissful quality of the soul. We experience the feeling of pleasure because of this Kosh. When you are in deep sleep (when your Manomaya and Vigyanmaya are often inactive), at times you experience extreme pleasure when you wake up. Such pleasure is being experienced because of the Aanandamaya Kosh.

The first 2 Kosh or layers (Anamaya Kosh and Pranayama Kosh) are called **Gross body** or the Sthula Sharira. This is the body that is left on this earth when someone lies, so the physical structure and the life air stays within the same earth or nature. This is something we can see or experience. Once someone dies, the soul along with the other 3 inner layers moves up the space to find its next chapter or journey of life. You may call it next life or reincarnation.

The Manomaya Kosh and Vigyanmaya Kosh together are also referred to as the **Subtle body** or the sukshma Sharira. It means something which we cannot see with our naked eyes. The footprints of our life and our all actions are stored here (the book of our karma, good or bad whatever it may be). The next birth (or yoni) is decided by this karma book and our soul is on the hunt for a suitable body that matches the karma. The soul and the body hunting game continues till the soul gets the purifications i.e., the person becomes blissful with purification of all karma. Once the soul is free from all the external sheath or layers, it gets liberation which we also call Mukti or liberation.

Our different body shapes of 8.4 million yonis (reincarnations) are due to the never-ending desires of our body. The body desires things not the soul. The soul is similar to the Super Soul/Almighty who is just playing the role of witness and guide. The soul does not get influenced or impacted by the body.

This is similar to the example of space. The space holds everything, but yet remains unaffected because it is subtler/lighter than the gross objects it holds. Similarly, the soul is the subtler energy. It remains its divinity even while it identifies with the material energy. The body, mind, ego and ignorance create confusion in us. (The body and Maya are the reasons). The soul is not impacted by anything, anywhere, anytime. Soul gets punished because it allowed the body to tilt towards impurities and failed to train it.

Those who understand the difference between the Kshetra (body) and kshetragya(soul) and the process of freedom from the material nature (by understanding the real knowledge) attain the supreme destination i.e., liberation.

Here is a learning and quick reference for this chapter: -

- Body and soul are different. The body is made up of 24 elements including mind, intellect, ego, unmanifested qualities of Prakriti, 5 knowledge senses, 5 working senses, 5 mahabhoot and 5 sense objects
- The Prakriti is the eternal energy that covers all the universes and has some minuscule portion present within our body. Prakriti is also referred to as Maya or material energy.
- Both the soul and Prakriti are the eternal part of God. They both are different energies
- Our body gets attracted to the Maya to experience the pleasure. Happiness, pain, greed, desires, etc are the qualities the body looks for in mother nature. All is due to the illusion created by Maya. Due to this we develop ignorance
- Our real knowledge to understand the difference between Soul and body. When this knowledge gets blurred, we associate ourselves as bodies rather than a Soul
- All our suffering is because of ignorance. We forget our purpose in life. We forget that this birth or life is given for purification of ourselves and to get rid of all the illusions and attractions of Maya
- Our body (which performs the karma) gets distracted in the physical world and seeks to achieve dominance over the material objects. We get

misguided and lose our focus on our objectives in life

- Our soul is the purest form of God. In a real sense, we should attempt to make our body (which includes our mind and intellect) powerful to learn the divine knowledge with the closeness of the divine soul. However, our ego (again part of the body) and the influence of mother nature, derail us from the spiritual path and we get trapped in this world
- We take birth after birth, due to our desires or pending wishes. God is kind enough to get us opportunities to fulfill our desires. We take up to 8.4 million birth and rebirth. However, the cycle of birth and rebirth is painful. One can never get peace or liberation without understanding the divine knowledge
- Our soul continuously guides us, our body but we ignore those signals. We hardly blame our karma or actions. The soul gets the punishment due to our poor actions in current life. God views it as the inability of the Kshetragya(soul) to guide the Kshetra (body). And the next body or life is based on the level of impurity that we have accumulated over rebirths. The soul is being made to change clothes (bodies) so as to keep guiding the new body repeatedly till liberation is achieved by human
- Soul remains as a witness in our hearts and guides us. When our body gets weak and near the destruction stage, we die due to aging or illness. The soul does not get influenced by our body or its actions. The soul is a portion of the eternal energy of God.
- Since we have some pending desire in our life, and we are impure too due to our bad karma, God gives us another chance to purify ourselves and learn divinity lessons to attain liberation. But we again ignore it. Only a few people, get the mastery of spirituality.
- However, once you understand the difference between body, soul, Prakriti, we get the real knowledge and our acts align towards self-purification such people are never reborn and attain liberation
- Our soul is an observer and witnesses our karma or actions during this life. And when we die, our soul as a witness, along with the supreme soul (Almighty) decides if we are pure or impure and if we need a rebirth. Our past and current karma, desires and purity decides our next birth
- We must continuously learn and make our life meaningful and stive towards achieving the liberation

CHAPTER XV

How our behavior changes with the qualities of Prakriti

Each of us behaves differently to different situations. Few are calm and composed while others are anxious, fearful, angry and confused. We often think it happens is because of our inability to deal with situations but in reality, that is not the case. As a human, we all are able and capable of managing situations but few of us have more influence of mother nature (Prakriti) on our body and mind. Many of us do not understand this mystery and the power of Maya behind the scene that makes us behave differently.

Everything under this universe is created because of the union of consciousness (soul) and the material energy of Prakriti (Maya). God is the creator of the universe including Prakriti. You may assume it as the Prakriti being the mother that gives birth to different bodies and species within her womb and the Almighty is the seed-giving father. The conciseness is the soul which is referred to here as the seed here whereas our body is referred to as the different species that are born within the womb of mother nature. The life force comes from God whereas the body/structure is built by the Prakriti.

God has empowered Prakriti to control each and every species within nature. There is a constant impact of the different qualities of Prakriti on us all the time, every minute, every second. And that is the reason, we behave differently at different times, we have mood swings, we become happy at times and become sad all of a sudden. Many are not able to cope with their sadness, grief, etc and few even attempt suicide to end their lives. This is foolish. We need to understand this. This is the core supreme knowledge and if we get it, we will not crib in our life. We can become balanced in our thinking with this supreme knowledge. Let's understand it closely.

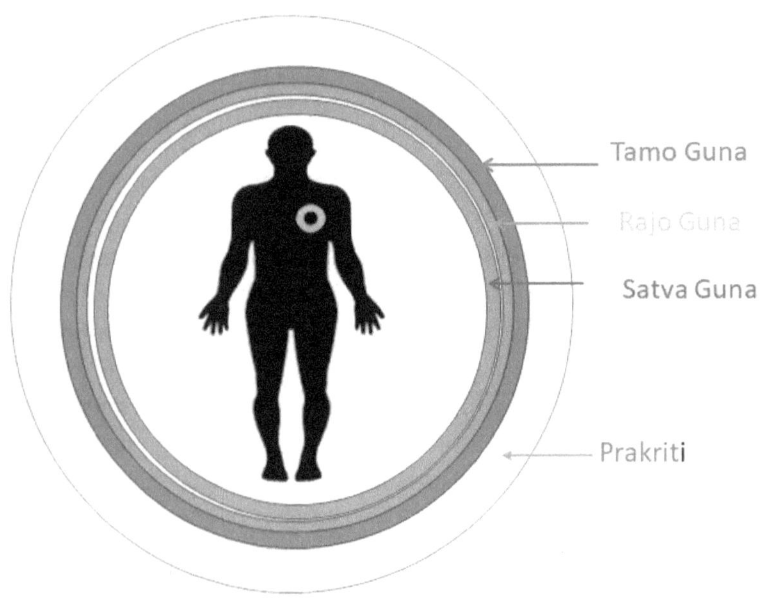

Understanding the impact of 3 qualities of nature on us

Prakriti has three powers viz Satva, Rajo and Tamo Guna within itself. These three Guna creates bondage in this world for all of us. Once the soul enters the Prakriti, it gets impacted and influenced by these Gunas (qualities of Prakriti). The Prakriti creates an illusion (Maya) around us that encloses the soul within itself and her captivity. The soul even being a divine power of God, immediately forgets its originality and its purpose and gets influenced by mother nature's qualities.

Both the soul and Prakriti (material energy) are divine forms of energy. However, Prakriti (Maya) is more powerful and has the ability to create illusions. When our soul gets in contact with the body, it loses its originality. This is similar to when our eyes are in contact with a color glass (of a spectacle), we see colored images from our eyes. When someone puts a dense black color speckle around our eyes, we see nothing. The eyes see the illusion created by the color glass. Our vision ability depends on the quality (color) of the spectacle we are wearing. There is an influence of it on our eyes. In similar ways, we (our body) have the influence of Prakriti (Maya) on us all the time. Maya creates illusion around us (similar to the spectacle) and we get influenced by Maya. We can nullify the influence of Maya on us with the power of spirituality. The illusion of Maya is due to her 3 qualities i.e., Satva, Rajo and Tamo Guna.

These 3 qualities make us do different things in life; we are dancing to the tune of these Gunas in our life. We fail to understand the impact of these guns and how to overcome or subdue their influence on us. This is the main reason for our attachment, our disappointments, our happiness, anger, greed and anything and everything in our life.

These Gunas are the reason for our attachment and pain in this world. Let's understand each of them

Satva Guna – This is also called Sato guna. It gives us true knowledge. It teaches us about taking care of our health, respecting others, and giving us the ability to differentiate between good and evil in life. It gives us happiness and wisdom in summary. Even though this is superior to other 2 gunas, it forces us to chase happiness continuously. This also creates a hunger for knowledge which can be dangerous too. You may not harm others but your hunger for happiness is never fulfilled. Your eagerness for knowledge develops the ego within you and you assume that you are better than others without realizing it. This may or may not reflect always it in your behavior but within yourself, you get a sense of pride in being more knowledgeable than others. This guna being the best amongst all, still has some impurity elements that are more like the side effect of knowledge and happiness.

Rajo Guna – This guna makes us chase worldly desires and affections and binds the soul through attachment to perform results-based-actions. It forces us to chase and continuously chase materialistic stuff in life. Chase for money, possession and materialistic gain are the attributes of this Guna. It inflames our desires for mental and physical pleasures. The majority of us are under the influence of this Guna. "I need more and more of this" or "I don't have enough" are the reflection of this guna within humans. The influence of this Guna is one of the prime reasons for the dissatisfaction in humans. The rat race for money/wealth, materialistic pleasure, affection/attraction/lust between genders can be attributed to this Guna. This puts us in a never unsatisfied category in this world. While there are many side effects of this guna, however, it forces humans to work hard and develops determination as a positive sign. At a broader level, this is the culprit for our dissatisfaction, disappointment, sadness and jealousy in this world.

Tamo Guna- This guna brings negativity and ignorance with us. This is a symbol of our carelessness, laziness, oversleeping, unpreparedness and lack of confidence. This faded our mind in such a way that we are not able to differentiate between good and evil. The violence, gambling, negative thoughts, lack of interest in anything and giving up or neglecting our duties and responsibilities, all are part of this Guna. Such people are not serious about life, lack determination, and do not perform meaningful actions as required by them.

All of these gunas have a regular influence on us all the time. Only one guna dominates at a particular time or phase. For example, when Tamo guna dominates us, the Rajo guna and Satva take a back seat or have little influence on us. Similarly, when Satva dominates, the Rajo and Tamo are suppressed.

When we die, the last state of our mind (the thoughts that are roaming in our mind just before our death) decides our next birth. People who die with Satva feeling are often reborn amongst the sages and higher abodes of the learned. People who die under the dominance of Rajo thoughts are reborn amongst the people driven by work and possessions whereas the people who die in the mode of Tamo guna dominance, take birth in the animal kingdom as an animal or insect species.

If you look closely, the actor or the doer is not you and me but rather the Guna. The Prakriti along with its guna is making us dance all the time. Those who do not understand it are fools. Those who get it knows that everything is under the grip of the guns. We must try to overcome the influence or effect of these gunas on us.

Lord supreme is beyond these gunas and once we get this divine knowledge, we become Tri-gunatit (beyond the gunas) and attain divine attributes similar to that of God. Once we get this, any influence of guna will not harm us or derail or distract us in life. In summary, we isolate ourselves from guns and their influence. We absorb the shocks of guna on us with self-control. This is a very difficult state to achieve. We have to give up our every attachment in this world, our attraction or affection to everyone whom we love, and must surrender to God to attain this state. By transcending the three guns (once we become Trigunatit), one can become free from birth, death, old age and misery and attains immortality.

What are the qualities of a person who is Tri-gunatit? Such a person is not impacted by anything in life. They neither hate any gunas nor carry any desire for it. They play a neutral role and understand that only the 3 Gunas are the active forces that are making us dance in life, so they stay established in self, in devotion without wavering.

Those who are alike in happiness and distress; who are established in self; who looks upon a clod, stone, and a piece of gold as of equal value; who remain the same and stable during pleasant and unpleasant events; who are intelligent, who accept both blame and praise in equal proportion, who remains same in honor and dishonor; who treats friend and foes alike and who have abandoned all the attachment driven activities, are the one called Gunatit, free from Guna's influence.

Those who serve God with complete devotion without any hesitation, rise above the three modes of material nature (beyond gunas) and come to the level of the Brahman, are the ones who get liberation.

Here is a learning and quick reference for this chapter: -

- The Prakriti has an ongoing influence on us every moment (every fraction of the time). Our behavior is driven based on the influence of the qualities of mother nature.
- The three guna or qualities of mother nature includes Satva, Rajo and Tamo. Satva is a symbol of knowledge; Rajo denotes attraction and attachment while Tamo represents ignorance and laziness. All guna have some degree of impurity. The Tamo guna is the most inferior guna whereas Satva guna is the supreme amongst all guns
- We are happy or sad based on our state of mind (part of our body). And mother nature has complete influence and control over our body which we hardly understand
- We must develop immunity against the influence of these gunas on us. The reason for our pain, sorrow and grief is the influence of these gunas on us.
- We must try to cross the influence of these gunas and develop a personality which is beyond these gunas (tri-gunatit). The one who does not get influenced by any gunas. This is the divine state of humans where you match the level of supremacy similar to that of God
- It is not easy to surpass gunas influence but with practice and devotion, we can always make an attempt to purify ourselves. We get peace with the spiritual journey
- Otherwise, we are forced into the cycle of birth, death, pain, sorrow, the endless loop which is not the purpose of our birth. We are not born to face challenges in life.
- We need to develop qualities of a Trigunatit which include becoming a better version of ourselves each day similar to a saint or a divine

personality who are alike in happiness and distress; who are established in self; who look upon a clod, stone, and a piece of gold as of equal value; who remains same and stable during pleasant and unpleasant events; who are intelligent, who accept both blame and praise in equal proportion, who remains same in honor and dishonor; who treats friend and foes alike and who have abandoned all the attachment driven activities, is the one called Gunatit, free from Guna's influence.

- Once we understand, the reasons, the cause and effect of the gunas on us, we can develop superior qualities to live a better life. Our behavior in different situations often represents our mental maturity.

CHAPTER XVI

Understanding our spiritual dilemma

The world is constantly changing. Because of the changes we strive in this world to survive, thrive and excel. But how well do we know this world in reality? We know it from a physical and geographical perspective but not much from a spiritual lens. Till now, we have learned in earlier chapters about we being always under the influence of Maya (Prakriti). Maya creates an illusion, so the world that we see as-is is not a real image, it is rather a reflection of it. This may sound weird but it is a spiritual truth.

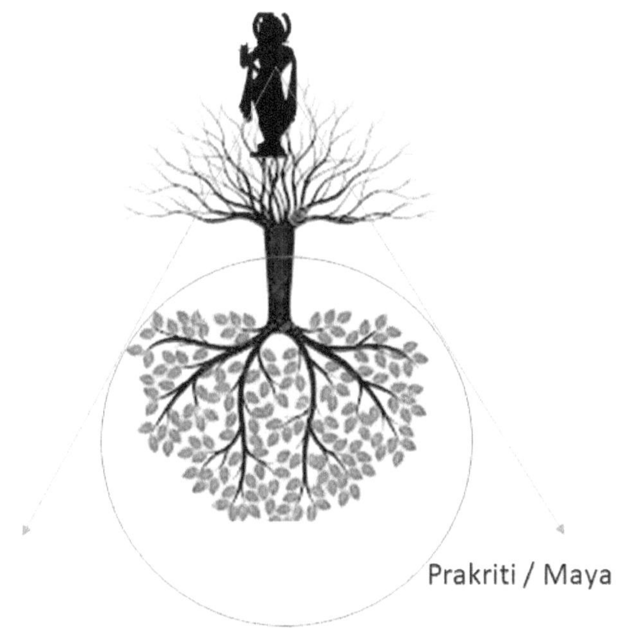

Understanding the world from a spiritual lens

In Bhagavad Gita, the world is referred similarly to as an "inverted" Banyan tree that constantly grows and changes. The roots of this tree grow upwards whereas the branches are leaning downwards. You may visualize a similar reflection of a real tree near the bank of a river (in the water). And you will see an image similar to what is shown here. The world is also a reflection of Maya. Whatever you see is just an illusion caused by the Prakriti. The leaves of the tree are the subjects/fruit that we constantly chase in this world (money/wealth, position, etc). And the branches and truck appear to be going up and downwards, similar to we develop a false sense of making progress in our life. You can also relate it to the ups and downs in our life due to our chase for subjects.

We can never understand this world in reality, as all we are seeing is a reflection. We have to cross it (cross the Maya influence) to see the reality. We will never come to know about its start, end, or base of it due to our ignorance. Our attachments are towards the subjects (leaves and fruits of the tree) in this world. We make efforts and put hard work to grab the fruits/leaves from this tree (world). Only with the knowledge and with surrender to God, we can understand this world. Once we get it, we would know the reasons for our pain. Those who get this understanding will make efforts to move towards the detachment in this world and will relate and accept to the power of the lord supreme who is running every activity in this world. We must chase the lord supreme, not the Maya nor the subjects of this world. It is the choice of picking between Maya or The God. Again, we have the freedom to choose.

Those who are free from ego and have overcome the attachments and desires in this world, those who treat pleasure and pain similarly and those who are spiritual and want to devote themselves to the Almighty are the ones who attain God. Such people never take rebirth (never return to the material world again) and they live in the Paramdham (the supreme abode) forever. The Paramdham is not influenced by Maya, neither sun or moon, or fire can illuminate the Paramdham. It is illuminated by the divine glow of the Almighty which is thousands of times more powerful than the sun and all planets' combined lights put together.

It is the Maya that creates confusion and we as a soul forget our identity and purpose. Each soul is a fraction /fragment of the Almighty, so it has all qualities of God just that due to the influence of Maya, we are chasing unnecessary stuff in current life. The material nature forces the souls to struggle with the six senses including the mind.

As the air carries fragrance from one place to another, similarly, the embodied soul carries the mind and the senses with it, when it leaves the old body and enters the new one. In chapter 13, we have seen how the soul along with the subtle body/Sukshma Sharir and Karana Sharir, moves into a new life.

The ignorant people do not get this. They fail to understand the impact of Maya on us as well as how the soul resides in the body and how it remembers its past karma. Our purity of soul is the only qualifier for Mukti or liberation. As long as the soul is under the influence of Maya, it will continue to confuse us, distract us and make us chase unnecessary stuff. With our determination, service to God and devotion, we can get rid of this trap which is the main cause of our pain in this world. Spirituality can help. Spirituality helps you decode things that science and technology cannot and will never be able to decode. The secrets of life can only be learned with spirituality, not by science or technology.

It needs trust and belief. If we question everything, we will never get started on the spiritual path. Science and technology are simply not there to prove the existence of the soul or a world beyond this universe. Things that we do not see or cannot be seen, do not indicate the non-existence of things. (It is our limitations). Spiritual knowledge is beyond our imagination.

We cannot say, things that are not yet proven, do not exist. There are thousands of miracles that are witnessed in this world every day that we do not understand and cannot explain. The only answer is there is belief in the superpower who is doing it for us, for helping us. Surrender your intelligence and ego and the path to spirituality would emerge and open automatically. Otherwise, we need a severe shock in life where we are forced to surrender to God, to find the answer to the "Why" of life. If our past karma has some purity, we will get a spiritual kick in our lifetime, it is inevitable. God will continue to give us opportunities to get purified and Maya will continue to confuse us to make the right choices.

God is seated in heart of each of us. Science may refer to the heart as a simple pump (of atrium and ventricles) for blood supply in our body but it is beyond that in spirituality. We get our memory, knowledge as well as forgetfulness from God. God is the only one who knows the real meaning of Vedas in Hindu mythology and all the Veda refers to him are an attempt to understand the Almighty holistically.

There are two types of creations i.e., Kshar (perishable) and Akshar (imperishable). The perishable are all beings in the material realm. The imperishable is the liberated beings. Besides these, there is a supreme divine personality (the Almighty) who is an indestructible Supreme soul. He enters the world as the controller and supports all living beings.

Those who know God without doubt as the supreme divine personality truly have complete knowledge and they worship him with their whole being. This is the most secret principle of Vedic scriptures and those who get it are enlightened and all their efforts are fulfilled by God.

Here is a learning and quick reference for this chapter: -

- We learn things based on observations, facts and experience. Our perception changes from time to time. We know that greed, lust and expectations from others are bad for us still, we get attracted to them. Our pains never end in life, we need peace and we chase it in form of money or some other form of satisfaction.
- We forget that someone is controlling us, somewhere. Mother nature (Maya) is creating the illusion and making us dance to her tune. This material energy makes us develop desires (recall the 3 Guna's of mother nature). The world is a reflection not a reality
- No one has conquered the world, no one is immortal, and no one has achieved nirvana while living in this world. This world is a place of suffering, a place of greed. Place of lust that gives us momentary pleasure which we all are chasing all the times
- We have to cross this reflection (of Maya). Only then, we can see the reality. Spirituality is all about achieving purity (purity of mind, body and soul). Once we enter this world, the Maya covers our body, mind and soul with its influence or power. (Maya is the power of God and more powerful than our soul).
- With surrender to God and with service to everyone in this world, we can make start our spiritual journey. We must believe in God, otherwise, we can never make a start. Our ignorance will continue to distract us but with determination, belief and surrender, we can always stay on the path of spirituality
- We also know that without inner peace, there is no meaning to this life. The million, or billion dollars of money is pointless if it cannot buy us peace. The relations give momentary pleasure not peace. Everyone is chasing inner peace, this is reality. People may not admit it
- Real peace is within spirituality. In the end, no matter what you do, the convergence of everything is within spirituality. The end goal of life should be spirituality (ultimate peace)
- This world will continue to be a place of pain and suffering, it is being designed for it by the Maya. Maya herself gives you continuous hints on, not to look at unnecessary things within this material world, as it gives pain. Our pain and sufferings are the lessons given by Maya to get the

basics rights, change your objectives/perspective of life, the goal of life, and get inclined within (towards God). But we rarely get those signals.

- Our chase is to grab the possessions of Maya/World and claim our ownership of it (All those belong to Maya). And she will take it back from us. It is her possessions, her world and her ownership, we are a guest in this world. Guest cannot claim ownership of things
- Our ignorance and ego are to be blamed here. Everything is perishable in this material world. So, no point in chasing or establishing ownership here. It will be left behind
- We all know this very well. But still, ignore it because we believe in living in present and enjoying life. But often forget that there is a life, after this life too. We have to settle our karmic account. God is fair to everyone. So, no one will be spared
- Let's make an attempt to purify ourselves. Spirituality is the only avenue to make it happen. Our inner peace is within us, we are chasing it outside. We need to look inwards and find a God within us and with this belief, we can make a start on our spiritual path

Things that we or our eyesight cannot see do not prove that things are beyond our vision. The same applies to spirituality, things that science and technology cannot prove, do not mean it does not exist. This knowledge existed thousands of years ago in Vedic scriptures. Just because few intellectuals think those are not the legit evidence from the lens of technology and science, does not make it irrelevant.

Spirituality is a search for the ultimate meaning and purpose of life. It helps understand life holistically with an objective of attaining inner peace and building a direct connection with God.

CHAPTER XVII

Human Behavior: Good and Bad side of it

We all judge people all the time. We have a tendency to find shortcomings or faults in others and often carry an illusion of being perfect. Any human quality can be broadly categorized into two types: Saintly nature (good qualities) and Demoniac nature (bad qualities). The majority of us have a mix of it, so we are neither perfect nor completely tainted. And this is bad for us.

Purity of self is the objective of life. The cycle of birth and death is natural so are our pain and sufferings in life till we make ourselves pure. Krishna encourages us to develop saintly virtues and give up the demoniac qualities. Many of us do not know the qualities that make a human a divine personality. This is beyond our looks and physical appearance of us. There are over 25 qualities that make a human a divine or a saint alikepersonality. These includes:

Fearlessness	Purity of Mind	Spiritual Trust	Charity	Control of senses	Sacrifice
Austerity/ penances	Simplicity	Non-violence	Truthfulness	Absence of anger	Peacefulness
Restrain from fault finding	Compassion /Empathy	Absence of greed	Gentleness	Modesty	Lack of fickleness
Forgiveness	Patience	Purity	Lack of revenge/ enmity	Absence of vanity/self-importance	

Key qualities for divinity

The above qualities make a human a divine personality and we must strive to elevate ourselves to acquire and enhance these qualities. The absence of it, anyway makes us behave like a demon without us realizing it. In addition, people who possess qualities of hypocrisy, arrogance, conceit/ pride, anger, harshness, and ignorance are demonic in nature. The divine qualities make our liberation/Mukti easy whereas the demonic qualities trap us in this physical world of pain, suffering, death, and rebirth.

Those possessing a demonic nature do not understand which actions are proper and which are improper. Hence, they possess neither purity nor good conduct nor even truthfulness. Such people think, the world is without any absolute truth, without any basis, without any God and it is created merely from the combination of two sexes (intercourse) and no purpose other than sexual gratification.

The demonic personalities are obsessed with endless anxieties that end only with their death. Still, they are desperate for the gratification of desires and accumulation of wealth and assume it is the highest purpose of life. Such high ignorance is the reason for their pain in this life.

Such people are held in bondage to thousands of desires that are driven by their lust, greed, and anger and they strive to accumulate wealth by unjust means, all for the gratification of their senses.

The demonic people think they have accumulated so much wealth already that they can fulfill any of their desires. They think they can even accumulate more for tomorrow and work towards it. They are under the illusion that they are superior to others and can control others and kill or suppress their enemies (or others whom they dislike) with the power of wealth. They assume that no one is at par or as powerful and happier than them. Such people due to their ignorance are always deluded or misled. Such people are always under tremendous worry and never at peace. Their attachment to materialistic things and add to the gratification of sensuous pleasure, make them qualify for endless pain and suffering and they are thrown into the murkiest hell after death.

When the Tamo Guna amplifies, humans are not able to differentiate between right and wrong. Such ignorance often triggers the Raju guna and we develop attachment toward physical possessions in this materialistic world. In short, we fail to differentiate what is needed in life for a peaceful living. We start chasing wrong things, we chase wrong relations, and we develop affections on temporary things including relations and physical stuff in life. The satva guna, helps us make the right choice in life whereas Tamo and Raju Guna derail us from our path of liberation or Mukti. Those who get this will easily understand the reasons for their pain and suffering in this world. God has given us the freedom to choose things, even given intellect to pick the right things. It is just our ignorance that indirectly gives us pain and suffering and that we all are responsible for it personally. No one else is responsible for our poor state of mind or poor. Stop blaming others. Develop the intelligence and move on with life.

Blinded by ego, arrogance, desire, and anger, the demonic personality individual abuse God, who is present in their own body and the bodies of others. If we start, treating others with an understanding that there is an existence of God (which is a pure soul) within them, then our perspective towards people would automatically change. The problem with humans is that they assume that they are superior to others (indirectly God resides within the hearts of others). The ignorance and increase of Tamo Guna are the reasons for our suffering indirectly.

Such demonic people who are cruel, jealous, and hateful take rebirth in the womb of similar demonic personalities (creatures) after death and they always are stuck in the painful cycle of birth and rebirth in inferior yoni and fail to attain God.

3 check gates lead to the hell of self-destruction for the soul- **Lust, Anger, and Greed.** Therefore, one should abandon all three. Those who are free from it, endeavor for the welfare of their soul and thereby attain the supreme goal.

Here is a learning and quick reference for this chapter: -

- Our behavior is driven by our qualities. Many times, we do not know if anything is wrong with us. This is purely due to our ignorance.
- At a broad level, we know the difference between good and bad. But we fail to realize that our understanding of it is limited.
- We hardly focus on self-development and self-improvement. This happens because we think we are perfect and others are at fault. This is a common problem where we look outwards for assessment of things, without doing self-evaluation
- We can develop both divine and demonic qualities. Many of us have mixed qualities. And that is the reason, at times we are sensitive.
- Our behavior is driven based on the impact of Gunas on us. The impact of Tamo guna makes us cruel, selfish, cunning, and destructive. The three Gunas' dominance does not last forever.
- Tamo guna often triggers Rajo guna that makes us focus on amplifying our desires. And we start chasing accumulations full of our energy. We work extra hard to get things done in life to fulfill our desires. This may appear as good quality, but it is not. The desires are the main enemy that takes us towards self-destruction.

- With the trust and belief in God, even though we are impacted by Tamo and Rajo guna, we can start the path to spirituality. This happens because the Rajo guna helps to amplify our determination abilities. With that, we can start anything.
- Many of us have a mixed impact on Gunas, so we behave differently in different situations, with different people. We are sensitive with few, we care for few, we hate few (or more) and we are jealous (of few). This is all because of Satva, Rajo, and Tamo playing with us due to the impact of mother nature on our body and mind
- We must make some efforts to get rid of our demonic qualities. And develop the divine quality. Although the list of divine qualities is exhaustive, even if we pick a few, we are making self-improvement
- Self-destruction happens primarily due to Lust, anger, and greed. The lust here refers to the broader category of desire not just limited to the sexual context but rather the sensual context
- Once we realize that something is wrong with us with self-assessment, we still have the possibility of changing our behavior. If others point it out, we often get angry (due to hurt of our ego)
- Human behavior can be studied. We are good at studying others. It is high time; we must study ourselves. Life would become much more meaningful and enriching

CHAPTER XVIII

Identify right Faith, Food, Sacrifice, Austerity and Charity

We all have some faith (Sradha). Faith is an integral part of the human being. As indicated earlier, the Prakriti has an influence on humans all the time. The prakriti has 3 qualities (Satva guna, Rajo guna and Tamo guna). Our faiths are also driven based on the influence of the Prakriti and its qualities on us. So, the faiths are also of three types Satvik (pure), Rajasic(semi-pure), and Tamasic(impure). The people who say they do not believe in God (atheist) primarily carry Tamasic faith which is driven due to their ignorance. Our behavior or attractions are often reflected based on the faith that we carry. The Satvik personalities often worship God, the Rajasic personalities often worship the Yakshas and Rakshasa whereas the people with Tamo guna often worship ghosts and spirits due to their ignorance.

The worship which is not performed according to the scriptures is of no use. People often forget that there is a God inside each of us. And this body is a holy place where God resides. So, people who harm their body in the name of worship or adverse austerities such as long fasts, standing on one foot, or other forms of worship types, gain little benefit due to their arrogance, ego, desires, and attachment. Those who abuse and torture their own physical body indirectly are disrespecting the supreme soul who resides within the body. True worship is done without any desire or expectations to showcase true love and devotion to the lord supreme. Rest all is the tamasic or rajasic type of worship.

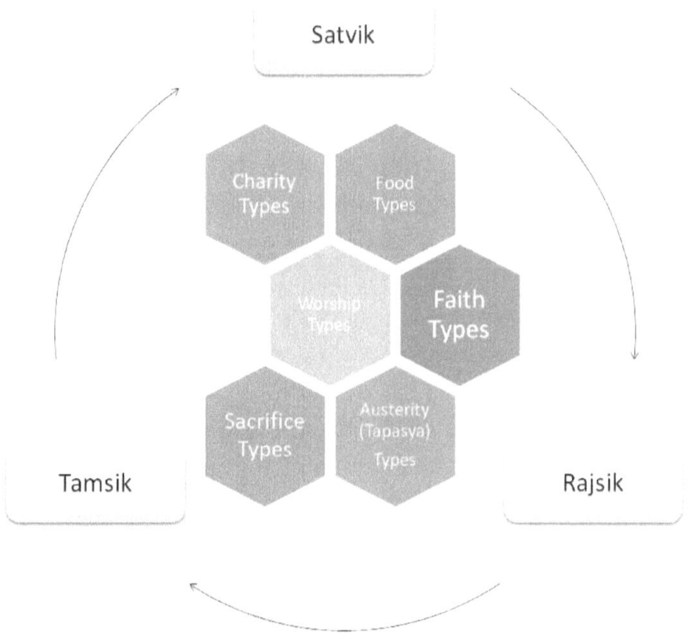

Understanding our Preferences

Mind and body often work in conjunction. Our faith influences our intellect (mind) and drives our preference for different food types for the requirement of the body. If a person is Satvik, he will never eat things that are either Tamasic or Rajasic in nature. So, Food is also divided into three types based on the qualities of Prakriti. Satvik food is nature given, juicy and gives purity of mind and heart, and promotes longevity of life. It includes grains, pulses, beans, fruits, vegetables, milk, and other vegetarian food. Foods that are too bitter, too sour, salty, very hot, pungent, and full of chilies are dear to the people who are Rajasic in nature. Such food (which is very tasty at the time of eating) often impacts our health and gives us pain, grief, and diseases later on. Food that is overcooked (within a period of three hours or more), stale, putrid, polluted, and impure is dear to the persons who are tamasic in nature.

Similarly, the sacrifice (aka Yagna) which is performed without any expectation of reward and done as a duty towards God, others, and society according to scriptural process is Satvik (pure) in nature. The sacrifice which is performed for material gain or with a hypocritical aim or ego is rajasic in nature. The sacrifice that is performed contrary to the scriptural process, without any mantra, chanting, and any donation or distribution of food or prasad is considered a tamasic sacrifice in nature. And such sacrifice is of no use to self and to society.

Austerity (Tapasya) is performed with 3 things i.e., **Body, Mind, and Speech**. Tapasya or austerity is performed for purity of mind, body, and speech. When we worship the Lord supreme, the Brahmins, the spiritual Master, the wise, and the elders with an objective of cleanliness, simplicity, celibacy (being unmarried), and non-violence is called austerity of body. Similarly, the Words that do not cause distress, are truthful, inoffensive, and beneficial as well as regular recitation of Vedic scriptures is declared as the austerity of speech. Similarly, serenity or tranquillity of thoughts, gentleness, silence, self-control, and purity of purpose are declared as the austerity of the mind.

Austerity which is without any gain or expectations keeping all the above three types of austerity (body, mind, and speech) is called Satvik austerity. The austerity that is performed for the sake of gaining honor or respect with ego for attention or ostentation or show-off is called Rajasic austerity. Its benefits are unstable and transitory. The austerity that is performed with an intention of harming others is called Tamsic austerity. Similarly, the Charity is also of three types i.e., Satvik, Tamsik and Rajsik. Let's explore them briefly.

Charity given to the worthy person (the one who really needs it or deserves it) without any consideration of anything in return, at a proper time in a proper place is stated as the Satvik charity. Charity is good for human beings, it helps to reduce our attachment, develops an attitude of service, and fosters sentiments of compassion for others. Charity given with reluctance, with the hope of a return or in expectation of a reward, is called the Rajasic charity. The charity which is given to the wrong person at the wrong time and at the wrong place without showing any respect or with contempt is called Tamasic charity.

"Om Tat Sat" is the first expression used by the first soul (also called Lord Brahma in Hindu scripture) whom Almighty to offer respect and prayer to the lord supreme. Om is the symbolic representation of the Almighty also called formless Brahman and is the primordial sound that pervades the creation (Om Tat Sat= Om (Almighty) Tat (the one who is pure) and Saat (eternal). And in Vedic scriptures, "Om Tat Sat" has become an expression of pure devotion to God. All the Yagna (Sacrifices), Tapa (Austerity), and Charity (Daan) must be done with purity and devoted to the Almighty and we must chant "Om Tat Sat" while performing any of these duties.

Everyone who does not expect any results in return and looking for liberation from this world must perform sacrifice, Austerity, and Charity while performing such duties by chanting "Om tat sat". Such duties are referred to as Tat (pure) that are associated with the lord supreme. The ultimate destination is also referred to as "Sat" (eternal) which is the lord supreme, hence any act such as Yagna (Sacrifice), Tapa (Austerity), and Daan (Charity) that are done for the lord supreme also becomes "Sat" in nature. The idea is not to think too much about which word to chant (Om or Tat or Saat", all represent the lord supreme only. So, all we need is pure devotion. Without faith, any of these (Sacrifice, Austerity, and Charity) become "Asat" which may be termed as impure or transient. And such Asat aspects are of not use both in this world or any other world across universes.

Here is a learning and quick reference for this chapter: -

- Mother nature or Prakriti influences each of us and there is an impact of Satva, Rajo, and Tamo guna on each of us all the time. We change our behavior because of the impact of these Gunas on our body
- Our actions are also driven by per influence of Prakriti. Our faith is driven by it. Food preferences are also governed by it.
- As we know the Satva is a better state compared to the Tamo and Raju guna so we all must strive to develop purity which is reflected in the Satva Guna
- For attaining God, we have to cross all these 3 gunas and become a "Trigunateet", the personality beyond these gunas which takes us to the same level as that of the Almighty. Reaching this state is extremely difficult
- Our karma should be devoted to getting ourselves free from attachments (Kaam (desire), Krodh (anger), and Lobh (Greed) as we have seen in earlier chapters.
- When we become selfless, we start performing duties for others' welfare. This is an elevated state of human
- The duties that are done for others can be performed using Yagna (Sacrifice), Tapa (Austerity), and Daan (Charity). These also influence

Prakriti, so we should strive for the Satva (top) quality of these duties that would make us ego-free, greed-free, lust-free, and anger free. In short, with this approach, we are developing purity for self

- Once we get pure; we are ready to serve God. With impurity, we are forced to take a circular path of birth and death and can never attain liberation or Mukti

- "Om tat sat" is the expression to worship God. Om is the primordial sound that pervades creation (Om tat Sat= Om (Almighty) tat (the pure one) and Saat (eternal) is the simplest expansion of this. We may use any of these words to express our love, respect, and devotion to God. This gives liberation. What matters is devotion.

- When our duties (Tap, Yagna, and Daan) become selfless, they become Saat in nature. i.e., as pure as God. The almighty is the purest of all. He is beyond all these qualities. He has created them.

- When our duties are driven by self-satisfying greed or desire, they become "Asat" also referred to as impure. Such efforts are a waste in this and the next birth as well.

CHAPTER XIX

The Ultimate Gyan and Conclusion

We often do not believe in the Saints, mythology, and spirituality people. Our brain is being designed to question and doubt everything around us. Life is meaningless if it is without trust and belief. We must understand how a belief system works (which is covered in detail in the next chapter).

We have to believe in something. When curiosity is coupled with experiences or evidence, we start trusting things. Spirituality is a belief system that can be experienced, felt, and practiced. The inner state of a human is very disturbed today to a level where people do not know what is right and what is wrong for them in life. Inner peace is missing in many of us. Bhagavad Gita has answers to everything. We have learned in previous chapters various things ranging from Managing emotions, managing self, doing our selfless duties, using intellect to overcome confusion, understanding the influence of nature or Prakriti on us and how to deal with it, and the qualities that we need to develop to live a dignified life. We also gained insights into the power of God, the illusions of Maya, and other important aspects. So far, we have learned, what not to do. Now let's look at what kind of karma must be done as must or mandatory karma.

We must make ourselves immune to outcomes or results. We do not control outcomes however we must do our duties with honesty. When we relinquish the fruits of all our actions, it is called a Tyag or renounced. Few intellects advise us to give up the karma or actions that trigger desires. Such selective karma is referred to as "Sanyasa". However, it is very difficult to pick and choose things that create bondages. Our intellect is not matured to a level where we can easily pick the right things that develop bondage. Neither, it is possible to give up all our karma or actions to avoid any kind of attachment. The food we eat, the air we inhale, and the words that we speak are also karma or actions that no one can give up in life. So, the best way to develop maturity in spirituality is by giving up the fruits of all our karma. Sanyasa indicates isolating yourself from society (renunciation of material desires) whereas Tyag means giving up fruits of all our karma so that we become immune to any situation.

Now the question comes of what kind of karma should never be given up in life. Krishna advises us to perform Sacrifice (Yagna), Charity (Daan),

101

and penance (Tapa) all the time as our duties. These must for done for the purification of the soul. And such karma must be done without any attachment, desires, or expectations.

Our real duty in life is to serve God. But we cannot just do that alone as we are also stuck in the social bondages. So, we must perform both till we get a complete realization. With spirituality, one can develop an intellect to a higher level and once that is attained, the bhakti (devotion) to God automatically develops and amplifies. It does not mean you give up your duties for your family and society. But for service to God, you need purity. And without the purity of our soul, God does not allow us to serve him, so we must get rid of the impurities within us. Otherwise, we know the bondages of life, the cycle of birth and death that invites endless suffering are unavoidable. The Mukti or liberation can be achieved with Bhakti which is devotion to God.

One may argue why we need liberation or Mukti? This is a silly question as that indicates people are ready to face the endless pain and ready to suffer in this life and life afterward. We are doing the work under the illusion of Maya or mother nature (Prakriti) but we mistakenly assume that we are the doers. Even mother nature operates on the instruction of God but it's our ego that corrupts our mind. Those who know this part, understand well that everything is being driven by God and they have no real role in this world, they are not the doers rather mother nature is the doer.

Our **knowledge** is also influenced by mother Prakriti (recall the three gunas i.e., Satva, Rajo or rajas, and Tamo or tamas). So, when we see God in everyone or every soul around us, our knowledge becomes divine. With such knowledge, we do not differentiate anyone, we do not insult anyone, and we are not fearful of anyone. We relate everything as a soul once our knowledge matures. The soul is eternal whereas the body is perishable, we know it very well. When we differentiate different people with different religions, races, creeds, skin color, social status, etc, it reflects our ego (of the superior complex) and reflects our rajas (Rajo gunas) type of knowledge. The knowledge which is neither logical, fragmented, and not based on absolute truth is called the tamasic knowledge. People with Tamsic knowledge declare themselves as God or the messenger of God. We have seen enough such conmen in our society. Similar our duties are also of categories of Satvik, Rajasic, and Tamasic types.

Duties or actions that are performed without any desires and attachment, without any expectations of reward, and without hatred are referred to as Satvik duty or karma. The duty that is driven by selfish desire, and ego and performed under stress is called rajasic karma. Actions that are intended to harm others (physical, financial, or mental) and performed without thinking or worrying about the consequence is referred to as tamasic karma. The performer of the duty can similarly be classified as Satvik, rajasic, or tamasic performer (Karta). The tamasic Karta or person is often undisciplined, vulgar, stubborn, deceitful, lazy, and stressful.

Along similar lines, the **Willpower** (determination) of people can also be of Satvik, tamasic and rajasic types. Same are the types of the intellect of human beings. Everything is under the influence of Prakriti. We are forced by mother nature to perform our duties based on the level of our knowledge and intellect. This can be elevated so is the case with the character of humans. By default, we have a natural or default guna that we inherit during our birth, however, we can change our guna as per our willpower, our interest level, and our preferences. We have full freedom given by God to pick our karma (but within the boundary and limits of mother nature). *It is our inability and ignorance which forces us to make wrong choices in life. And we get punished for it as well.* It is similar to a situation where a mother is trying to punish a child to rectify his or her mistakes. Prakriti performs the same role. The only guiding rule here is to perform our duties with honesty and selflessness.

No duty is ugly or impure, the consciousness with which we perform it determines its worth. Our duties (responsibilities) come naturally to us. We must do our duties and not judge it to assess if it is impure or defective. Abandoning our assigned duties and taking on other duties/responsibilities (assuming something else is relatively easy or better or superior) does not come very naturally to humans. This is due to our personality and the level of qualities we possess. The simple example here is about Arjuna who was a warrior (and his duty is to fight injustice, and protect his country, and in that process even if he kills people during the war or sacrifices his own life that is considered a part of the duty of a warrior). But when the time came to fight his unjust family members, he became emotional and preferred to run away or become a saint. This happened due to his ignorance.

Along similar lines, we are born with a tag or religion, or category. And we often pick the duties based on our comfort, expertise, and other elements that influence us. Few become priests or pandit due to their knowledge or interest whereas few become businessmen, few prefer serving the society as a nurse or doctor or a cobbler whereas few prefer to pick the duty of soldiers to serve the nation. These are natural transitions. We cannot switch our duties or act abruptly.

Even if we want to, mother nature will test us till we develop a quality that fulfills or qualify the needs for a specific role or a profession. Doing duties honestly, and commitment is what defines our character.

No matter what duty we are doing today, there are impurities in them. One of the main impurities that we carry is not doing any of our duties towards God. Our duties are driven by the selfish motto. None of us have 100% Satvik qualities otherwise we would have already been on the path of devotion, without any worry, or expectations. But we all are disturbed in some of the other forms. Bhagavad Gita indicated that surrender your every action to God and with devotion, you can develop divine knowledge and ultimately attain divine god. So, our ultimate aim or purpose of life should be God nothing else as all routes of the path of life end at the Almighty. No point in running around the materialist stuff, it creates pain, and dissatisfaction and makes us further impure. We have learned it very clearly till now in this book.

We need faith in God and with that, in every difficult situation we can come out. God will guide us and take care of us. We need this belief. Ups and downs are inevitable in life. We must not lose our character but rather glorify it with selflessness, care, respect for everyone, and devotion to God. The ultimate peace is not in this world but within ourselves. And the principles of the Bhagavad Gita help us achieve inner peace with ease.

Today, we have the freedom to choose. We may give up essential duties or pick the duties as per what we like or dislike. This makes us get trapped in this material world to dance to the tune of mother nature invites pain, grief, and endless struggle. We must do our dharma (or duties). Many do not get the dharma definition of the Gita. It essentially points to material dharma and spiritual dharma.

In the material dharma, we all are playing various roles such as father, mother brother, sister, husband, wife, citizen, taxpayer, etc in this material world. We must do this dharma (material dharma) with honesty and as per the rule book of Gita which says do not get into attachments, bondages but do your duties holistically without any expectations, without any other regrets. This is the elevated state of our intellect that helps us to do our material dharma.

On other hand, the spiritual dharma relates to our duty towards the world i.e., every soul. In this, we identify ourselves and others as souls, so we have duties towards every other soul in this world. Respect, care, love, and affection for everyone are some basic qualities that we need here. There are no other relations that exist in spiritual dharma as everyone is identified by soul. And all our services are for God who is sitting in everyone's heart, so indirectly we are servicing God. We must give up Kaam (Desire), Krodh (Anger), Lobh (Greed), Mohr (attachment), and Ahankaar (ego). These are the basic requirements for performing the true dharma or duties. Once we develop the mastery of material dharma, the transition to spiritual dharma becomes a bit easier.

The material world to a spiritual world journey is difficult but with trust and faith in God, this can be achieved. If we think, this path is difficult, another simple approach is to surrender everything to God. This is the supreme Dharma. Make God the reason for everything. Once we make a start in this righteous path, we are guaranteed to attain God. A true devotee does not desire Moksha or Mukti, he just aims for the blessing and companionship of God.

One must revise the learnings from Gita from time to time and practice the same. We must also share this knowledge with others who are eager to learn or have the curiosity to understand spirituality. The purity in Geeta will bring Mukti or liberation to every human who picks the path of devotion. This helps both the people who learn it and who listen to it to get rid of their sins and attain the divine abode of Lord Krishna.

Here is a learning and quick reference for this chapter: -

- Sanyasa involves isolating ourselves from society (renunciation of material desires) whereas Tyag refers to giving up fruits of all our karma while dealing with society. While both require sacrifice, between these two, Tyag is superior
- We must never give up karma of Sacrifice (Yagna), Charity (Daan), and penance (Tapa) in our life. These karmas are mandatory in life to purify ourselves
- Spirituality strengthens our intellectual maturity. We get an understanding of the reasons for our pain and suffering. And get an understanding of our existence and our purpose in life which is to develop purity of self (removal of critical bad qualities) and develop devotion toward God
- The reason for our pain is driven because of nature or Prakriti and the only savior for us is the Almighty. All our paths of life end at God, so in

end, no matter what we do in life, we are forced to move towards him either due to our death or post-liberation. (He is the one who created us and everything around us)

- Those who understand life, develop devotion, enhance their belief and get into the spiritual path as per their different life situation, experiences
- Our Knowledge, Duty, and Willpower are influenced by mother nature's quality (Satva, Rajo, and Tamo). They are interlinked and influence our life. Each of them can be Satvik, Rajsik, and Tamasic in nature. We need the right knowledge to do our right duty and the willpower to face challenges while performing our duties.
- We must perform our duties with honesty without any desires and attachment, without any expectations of reward, and without hatred treating it as our Dharma (rigorous act)
- Our duties will have continuous influence by mother nature and it would take our exams from time to time (in form of ups and downs in life) to check our eligibility for our divine qualities
- The influence of mother nature would give us the realization of how pain and suffering are developed in life and how to make ourselves immune to it
- We have to perform the materialistic Dharma or duty (the duty towards our relations) as per the role God has assigned to us such as father, mother, brother, sister, etc at the time of our birth
- In addition, we have spiritual dharma as well which is our duty towards other spirits (every soul within this world), we have a spiritual connection with all of them. They all carry the same portion of God (soul) within them as we carry.
- Our duty (dharma) towards them should include respect, care, love, and affection for everyone are some basic qualities that we need here.
- Our duties towards God and other souls/individuals should be the same. As they are the same. This is true knowledge that we miss because we identify ourselves as a body and not as a soul. We need faith
- Spirituality is about faith and devotion to the Almighty. This is the divine knowledge that summarizes Bhagavad Gita
- Once we realize that everyone is a soul and has the same power (God) within them. The companions, expectations, etc do not apply.
- Spirituality helps to understand life much better. We need trust and belief to start our spiritual journey.

- We must devote ourselves to God (irrespective of our religion) and start practicing things that would make our life easy without causing any harm to anyone.
- In end, if we get liberation or not, is not important. What matters the most is we are not wasting this life (in pain and suffering) which is given by God as a precious gift for a much broader purpose which is the purification of self.
- Let's start spirituality to give us inner peace which we all are missing today.

CHAPTER XX

Understanding Our Belief System

A belief is something we consider to be a fact. It is anything that we assume to be true. We use our beliefs to understand and navigate this world. As we mature, our personal experiences that are repetitive and our inference helps us either firm such belief or change our belief to something else.

Beliefs are personal. so, you should never question someone's belief to be right and wrong. It is an individual's validation and affirmation from this real world as per what they feel, experience and infer from it. Once formed, these beliefs become ingrained in us. We take them for granted, and we also assume our beliefs to be factual, whether they are true or not.

Belief formation starts when we are small children. Whatever our parents teach us or tell us in the early stages of our life, becomes our belief largely. What our teachers tell us, we assume to be fact (another belief). The family, school life, college, and the environment around us help us to shape our initial beliefs.

Let's take an example here. If a child is a little fat in the early years, and her friends bully her for her body shape, she may start believing that she is ugly in looks. When she brings this topic with her parents, they may tell her to ignore such things and remind her that she is beautiful. In case, she gets bullied again in another place while playing with other kids a few more times, her belief of being fat and ugly gets stronger. She may either develop an inferiority complex and may not carry herself naturally in social places. Her belief of being ugly is not true (as for children, our bodies undergo continuous changes). Another example is, if as a child, we perform poorly in maths exams, our teacher tells us that we are weak in maths. And we accept it as fact. The reality could be different (e.g., we did not stud or were unwell on the day of the exam or something else) but our belief in what the teacher told us and fear of math will stay with us lifelong. Our belief system makes us carry the message of maths being a tough subject for our entire life.

Our beliefs determine if we consider something or someone to be good or bad, right or wrong, beautiful or ugly, desirable or undesirable, safe or dangerous, worthy or unworthy, or acceptable or unacceptable. Our beliefs also dictate what we consider to be possible or achievable. The good news is our belief system can change based on our thoughts, our intellects, our learnings, and our experiences during our entire life.

The classic example is learning spirituality. Very few of us learn or master or practice spirituality during our early days of life and after that, we get busy in life. So, there is a common belief that spirituality is for old people.

Once we grow and experience life, we feel a strong need for it. Our thoughts mature, our experiences glow and we get different realities of life which inspires us to learn the unknowns or at least get some reading/ learning around it. When we find it meaningful, relate to it ourselves, and experience it, such things change our beliefs. And the inclination develops on such a subject. There is nothing wrong if someone practicing it or not, it is based on how our mind perceives things.

The belief is stored in our subconscious mind and acts as an automatic response system of our brain. Our beliefs affect our behavior, thoughts, and emotions. So, it is a bit difficult to change the belief system in many once it becomes firm and thick within our minds. Childhood beliefs of severe fear, and hate is the most difficult to change at later stages.

Beliefs can empower or limit our capabilities. Limiting or negative beliefs prevent us from fulfilling our true potential, holds us back, and give rise to negative thoughts and emotions. Empowering or positive beliefs, on the other hand, allows us to act resiliently, believe in ourselves, and invoke positive thoughts and emotions.

Let's understand how the belief can either empower or limit our capabilities and how it can either help or harm us with a few examples: -

Limiting belief	Empowering Belief
I need to be wealthy to be happy	I can choose to be happy no matter what the circumstances
My body type is such that I cannot lose weight no matter what I do	I can be slim and healthy if I exercise regularly and eat right
My family background limits what I can become in life	I can become anything I want to with the proper training and effort
I cannot start a business because I do not have the initial capital	I can start a business by meeting the right people and getting an investor
I will never find the right person for me and get married	The right person for me is out there. I simply need to get out and meet people
Most people are dishonest and out to cheat me	The majority of people are honest and kind
Their religion is not good. It teaches violence and cruelty	All religion teaches peace and harmony. It is individual behaviour that cannot be attached to religion

Our beliefs govern our Life

Let's respect people with different beliefs, religion, their preferences. The spiritual inclination is driven based on belief. At some point in time during our life, many of us would develop our intellect to appreciate spirituality. And this helps for mental peace. It is already proven by science and research. So, it is no longer a question for debate!

CHAPTER XXI

Hundred Golden Questions & their Answers for inner peace

Our life throws many challenges at us and put us into awkward situations. Many times, we do not know what to do and whom to approach as we ourselves are struggling with our life. This question bank covers the most questions many of us face in life from time to time where we question our capabilities, people around us, God, Spirituality and everything around us. This will help answer your key questions about life. It has 100 questions and their answers that are classified into 10 different categories such as

1. Self Doubt
2. Family & Relationship
3. Managing Emotions
4. Profession
5. Fame, Position and Money
6. Depression
7. Death
8. Spirituality
9. Different faith and Gods
10. Soul

SELF-DOUBT

1. Why I am not very successful in life? What is that I am missing within me?

Your question clearly indicates you are lacking self-confidence. We all are perfect. God has created each of us for a reason. Don't consider life as a burden or a race. With such a mindset, no one can enjoy life. Noting is missing or lacking in you. We have a beautiful mind. And when it goes against us, it becomes our enemy. It produces negative thoughts and emotions. Try to befriend your mind, with your thoughts. Trust in yourself and your capabilities. Things will settle automatically. Success is a relative term. Material success should never be the yardstick of life. You should not chase success but rather look for peace. Once you get peace, you will automatically experience success. You must convince your mind and your definition of success would change.

2. Why do I continue to face challenges in my life?

Life in itself is a struggle for many. You are not alone here. We are born in this world to taste the bitterness of life and learn from it. Problems and challenges are inevitable for everyone. It is our ability to handle the challenges that define our character. We must learn to face difficulties and handle them. Learn to handle things better. Your challenges or trouble are driven based on your past karma, past life, your expectations from current life and your poor ability to handle failures. We all carry karmic bondages from previous life which we have to settle in this life. If your karmic balance is negative from your previous lives, you face more challenges and struggle in your current life compared to others. Stop comparing yourself with others. Your karma and their karma are different. In the worst case, convince your mind that your troubles are due to karmic balance and not due to your capabilities or efforts. Train your mind to accept that it is okay to have problems in life and there is a solution for every problem. The time changes and your time is yet to come, convince yourself with this thought.

3. My life is not perfect. God is not at all kind to me. What should I do?

Life does not have a shape that you can compare to judge its perfection. So, perfection or imperfections are not with life but rather with our thoughts and feelings. The purpose of life is to develop the purity of self. Which is nothing but purity of our mind, our intellect, our thoughts and emotions. Keep control of your negative thoughts that are giving you an impression of life not being perfect. No person can be a judge or decide if his or her life is perfect or not. Life is given by God and he cannot be a poor creator. Our life is perfect. We have made it imperfect with our actions, thoughts and accumulations. This applies to everyone. God is kind to everyone. He is an observer of our life who just witnesses what we are doing every moment. To get god's blessings one needs to surrender himself or herself to God. This does not mean, you become a saint or run away into mountains or jungles leaving all your relations and personal stuff. Surrender refers to the extreme love and trust in God where all actions are being aimed towards or done for God. Spirituality is the answer if you need the love of God. Learn it, practice it and develop mastery in it. That will give you peace of mind.

4. Why I am not able to handle things better than others? Am I worthless?

Your question indicates that your emotions have cluttered your mind. You are going through lots of negative emotions that give you a feeling that you are worthless. You need to manage your emotions. Negative emotions are more dangerous than wildfire. We all are the beautiful creation of God, so no one is worthless. If we were to be worthless, God would have never created us. So, stop such thoughts which are not relevant. Since you are carrying the feeling of self-worthlessness and self-doubt, you always find yourself at a lower rank than others. In simple words, you are always comparing yourself with others continuously, you are fearful of others, you are fearful of situations, and you are fearful of the outcome. It is your fear that is hurting you more than others. Stop blaming yourself for everything that is happening around you. You are a beautiful soul. No one in this world is perfect except God. You must learn to manage your emotions. Stop comparison with others. Such aspects only give pain. This applies to everyone. Build your self-confidence and you will see a much better picture.

5. I am attached to my family and do everything for them but they do not love me. Why it is so?

Your answer lies in the question itself. The biggest problem for you as well as for many of us is attachment. Attachment gives pain. Attachment creates desires, and expectations from others and when those are not fulfilled its gives anger and pain. Bhagavad Gita clearly states that if we can manage our attachment, we qualify for liberation otherwise pain and suffering are inevitable in our life. You must do your duties towards your family but do not keep any expectations from them in return. If they love you, this is a bonus otherwise don't get disheartened. Your relationship with your family members is due to the karmic connections of your past lives with them. So, if someone is not been kind to you, it is ok. It is their and your karmic qualities mismatch that is extending even in the current life and interfacing with each other. You should do your duties, and spread love and care. Your duties to your family members should not get compromised irrespective of what you get in return (in the form of love or neutral response or even negative response from them). You should do your duties, the rest all will fall in place sometime for sure. Have faith and trust in God.

6. I am giving 100% of my efforts, still, people think I am not giving the best. Why?

If you are facing such criticism regularly there could be two possible reasons. Either you are amongst the wrong set of people whose wavelength/ thinking does not align with yours or there is a possibility that you may be missing some of the skills or qualities which others are expecting from you. You must assess it honestly. You are the best judge to question yourself and challenge your core capabilities and skills. Identify what is wrong and address it accordingly. If it requires you to learn new things, please go for it.

7. I am not sure about my purpose. People keep telling us to have a purpose in life. Is it really necessary?

The purpose is a heavy word. It is often used as jargon in our society to show your weight and impress others. People often get confused between purpose and goal. And that is the reason many uses goal and purpose interchangeably. As per Bhagavad Gita, the purpose of our life should be liberation (purity of self to attain God). This is nothing but union with God.

The purpose can be materialistic as well as spiritual. The materialistic purpose gives pain and suffering whereas the spiritual purpose gives ultimate peace. So, you should choose your purpose wisely. Spiritual purpose takes us towards liberation. Liberation in simple terms indicates we getting permanent freedom from our pains and sufferings. In short, we are not reborn again in this world once we achieve liberation. Without purity of soul, we cannot attain liberation. God is very pure and does not accept any impurity. So, we must make attempts to purify ourselves. This includes purity of thoughts, body, mind and soul. In the end, the soul unites with the almighty which is the liberation state. Our pains are due to numerous cycles of birth and rebirth that we take in this world. This world is a place that gives us pain. It is a place that develops attractions, desires and attachments and traps us in the endless cycle of birth. At the same time, this world is the place that teaches us liberation and how to attain it. We must choose our purpose wisely. Here are the reasons why.

Purpose acts as fuel or motivation in life. It gives inspiration and zeal to face the difficulties and hardships in life. So having a purpose in life is very important. Many of us carry the materialistic purpose of what we want in life or what we want to achieve or become. E.g., someone wants to become a CEO, someone wants to be a billionaire someone wants to be a popular singer, etc. These all are the materialistic purposes. A true purpose cannot be self-driven or self-focused. The examples above are more like goals in life. The ultimate purpose for life for everyone should be liberation and union with God. But very few understand it or make it their purpose. If you care for your purpose, devote your life to others or to society without any expectations. Otherwise, chase your goals in name of purpose. That should suffice to live in this world.

8. I am fearful about the future. Not sure if I can face it. What should I do to overcome such fear?

Fear is natural to humans. We all are fearful of something or the other in life. Our biggest fear in life is the "fear of losing" something that we love and care. A few examples are wealth, money, status, relationship, family, etc. When life throws challenges at us, we get fearful. This is natural. This is due to our brain triggering the emotions of fear. Fear creates panic and negative thoughts in humans. And our inability to manage the panic makes us uncomfortable. We call it stress as well. It can be managed; emotions can be controlled with logical reasoning most of the time.

Fear cannot be removed or eliminated from our life but we can develop the courage to handle it or overcome it in specific situations. Learn from your experiences. Train your mind and remind yourself that it is okay to face fearful situations. Maintain a balance of mind. This is the best way to handle fear. Remind yourself about you are capable of handling the fear or the fearful situations. Develop the pattern of such thoughts in your mind so that your mind gets adjusted to handle fear. Mind is your friend as well as an enemy. Train it to handle anything in life. Another fear that we often worry about is the "fear of failure". We must remember that the outcome of many situations (in fact every situation) is not in our control. We can only control our efforts in life, not the outcome. So, failure is not in our hand anyways. Preparing ourselves for failures or the worst situation is another way to handle fear. Use your intellect to manage fear and leave the rest to God. You can also seek the advice of teachers and gurus who can teach you some spiritual ways of dealing with fear.

9. My luck is not favorable to me. This has been the case for many years? How long should I face life?

You seem to be disappointed with life. You must divert your mind toward spirituality first. Spirituality will help to calm down your noisy mind. You can start with basic meditations first. We all are born with some default luck quota (the good or bad baggage of our fortune from our previous life). This influences our current life. However, your efforts in this life should be your focus and you must align to the right things that create lesser bondage towards the world. You also need to accept that results are not in our hands, so do not measure everything on a basis of outcome. We all are doing this mistake and that is the reason for our disappointments and unhappiness. You need to be clear on what you are looking for in life. Fame, money and social status all are perishable and temporary so look for things that can give you real peace in mind.

Luck is favorable only to those who are born with it and others they must earn the luck in this life. This is achieved through our good actions and deeds. You must assess the reasons for your disappointment. Reading Bhagavad Gita can help. Meditation can help to understand life. Once you accept the variations in life, you will get clarity on what to do in life, how to manage disappointments, how to be happy, and how to hunt for the ultimate peace. Your problem is a common problem for the majority of people. When we face negative situations repeatedly, we are bound to develop a negative perspective toward life. But life is not being given to accumulating negative feelings but rather meant for learning, improvements, and doing things that can give pleasure and ultimate peace. Hunt for those peace elements in this world, the solution would automatically emerge. There is no point in cursing yourself or your life or your luck as that would never give you a solution. The solutions are within you (your soul), around you (nature, spirituality), and the people around you (find a guru or place to practice meditation). If all such things do not help, there is no harm in taking the help of a doctor who can help control your anxieties in life. Our brain is a chemical factory that produces hormones (happy and stress hormones) continuously, every moment. All we need is a method to control those negative hormones either through spirituality or through medical care. There are definitive solutions, so relax and enjoy life bit by bit.

10. It is often said that Spirituality requires sacrifice. Can we practice spirituality without changing our Lifestyles, jobs, or Profession or without leaving our families?

Spirituality is often mistaken as complete detachment from this world and running away from our existing relationships, people, and profession, and changing our lifestyle dramatically. This is not true. Spirituality is all about making attempts to make ourselves pure so that we can experience God (ultimate peace) around us, within the self. Even if you fail to see God, spirituality helps you to become a better human being. It controls our brain's noise to a great level which gives mental peace. With spirituality, you start respecting people, and their actions and develop intelligence and clarity towards life. Spirituality is mostly the mental alignment to convince yourself of various things which we often ignore in life including God. It is more to attain purification of self, mind, and body which ultimately results in purification of our soul energy.

There is no need to do any dramatic changes in life. People often assume sacrifice means giving up every relationship. In spirituality, sacrifice is related to the giving up wrong/immoral qualities of humans such as the sacrifice of greed, ego, lust, anger, attachments, desires, and fear. You can still do all your regular duties, work, etc as-is without any changes in life. However, you may need a dramatic change in your thinking process, in your faith and belief. This is more towards developing new cognitive capabilities so that can control your mind (e.g., meditation), and emotions to develop focus capabilities and faith in God. In spirituality, everything is related to energy be it soul or be it, God.

We are soul energy which is impure and God is the purest divine energy. Spirituality is a process that helps you develop purity within yourself so that you give up all your impurities in life and build a supreme level of purity similar to that of God. Once that happens, you get liberation. Your soul gets released and dissolves within the divine energy. You must read Bhagavad Gita or other spiritual literature in your life and apply some of those disciplines in your current life. It is not difficult to make a start.

FAMILY & RELATIONSHIP

11. I love my family and doing my duties honestly? But I think they do not value it. What is that I am missing?

This is a common problem in families. Especially ladies witness this problem the most. Many mothers are doing so much of sacrifice in their life but they still feel their work is not appreciated or valued. If you are doing your duties with complete honesty, then there is nothing that you can improve. You are doing justice to your role. Your problem is not with your duties but rather with the expectations from the family. You are expecting respect, appreciation, and care in return from your family. You may not say this explicitly but this is a common human expectation. You are doing a selfless duty but there is an element of expectation that is hurting you the most. As per Bhagavad Gita, expectations always give pain so you must isolate your duties and your expectations from your family. Once you stop expectations in return from your family, you will it be at peace.

These are the spiritual ways of addressing the problem which you stated. There is another method where you can use your intellect to assess if raising your concerns openly with your family is going to help or not in terms of calming down your mind. Even if you are not sure what to do, raise it once to express your state of mind with your family members openly. You must use patience and a calm tone to express yourself. Otherwise, you may ignite the ego and anger of your family members if they are not sensitive to feelings. Unfortunately, each human is different and they value different things. (Ego and Anger are common human traits that get ignited easily in people). Many times, our family members take things for granted, so unless you express and tell them what is bothering you, they will not care or in many cases may not even notice. This is the sad part but unfortunately, it is the reality in many families. You need to divert your mind to areas that can give you peace. There are other methods like exercise, swimming, walking, reading, etc which can divert your mind. If you want deep inner peace, then you must start with meditation and gradually develop your expertise in learning spirituality. Read Bhagavad Gita or similar books if you have a spiritual interest. This is an entirely personal choice. Many find spirituality as suffocation too as they are not able to understand where to start. And many give up it after a few tries. In such cases, you need to find a teacher who can guide and teach things in a step-by-step manner.

12. Is it necessary to get married and get stuck in life? Do we need a family or relationship in life?

Marriage is entirely a personal choice. God has given us the freedom to choose. You may choose to get married or stay single. One must be wondering what Bhagavad Gita says about marriage? The answer is more aligned to what is your purpose of getting married. There is no direct mention of marriage in the Bhagavad Gita however it does guide us on the purpose of our sexual orientations.

Family and relationships are largely driven based on our karmic relations of the past with different people. This may sound weird. But as per Bhagavad Gita, everything is happening as per the wish and order of God. So, the partner we get or the family we have, all are not because of our choices but rather as per our karmic activities of past and current life.

Marriage is considered as pious arrangement in Vedic scriptures as a token of love and blessing of God to start a family so that you can grow a child into a devotee. When sextual activities are undertaken only for sensual pleasure, it is considered as animalistic (even within a marriage). When the sextual acts are aligned with the dharma (righteous spiritual injunction) with consent of partner for a purpose to grow family), it becomes as pious.

13. I have a troublesome life with my spouse. s/he does not respect me or care for me. What should I do?

The compatibility issues are common amongst spouses and can be sorted with open dialogues and understanding of your partner. Life is all about respecting and caring for everyone (including your spouse). When we view people from a lens of spirituality, it is assessed not with the relationship angle but rather from a soul aspect is considered. Every soul belongs to God. And there is God (soul energy) within everyone (including your partner). So, both of you have divine qualities. There is soul energy which is indirectly the God who is sitting in our hearts (including that of your spouse). Unfortunately, none of you are realizing it and that is the reason for your troublesome life with your spouse. This is in addition to the differences (in thinking, preferences, choices, etc) that exist in every relationship.

You must talk to your spouse with a calm mind and express your feeling first to sort out the difference. Give it some time to settle. If this method does not work, you need a marriage counsellor (not spirituality) or someone whom both of you respect and admire to guide you. If the marriage has become really troublesome (violent, abusive in nature) and unbearable, you need not continue your suffocations. This is against the Dharma (righteous act). There are methods of separation which can be explored as a last resort if other attempts fail to save the marriage. The difference in marriages is common these days, and many can be sorted with open dialogues, openness to accept feedback, and with active listening.

14. We do not have kids. Kids are God's gift. Why God is being so rude to us?

Everything in the universe happens for a reason. God is the decision maker and arranger for everything. You have not indicated if you have consulted the doctor and undergone any treatment along with your spouse. There are various medical methods available to conceive. If you have not explored you may explore them too.

There is a soul in every human being. You can find a child in every child in this world. If you are open-minded, there are options to adopt a child as well. This is the best way to serve and help a little soul that is hunting for a helping hand. You may explore this option too. This is the best fulfillment one can have and a divine act to service god.

If none of the above options suits you, you need some counseling. God is not rude to anyone. He has given us the intellect to accept things. Everything cannot be explained with logic in this world as many things are done by God for our best interest which is beyond imaginations and explanation. If something is happening too bad in your life related to conceiving a baby, this may be due to your poor karmic account of the past life.

15. My kids do not give respect to me? How should I deal with it?

Kids learn over time. Their belief changes, interest level changes, and behavior too. You must have an open communication channel with your kids. Initial stages, kids learn what they observe and experience from parents, teachers, friends, and the environment in which they grow. Assess if your spouse is giving them the right coaching on their respective elders. If your partner is not kind or respectful, kids pick up such a trait and reflect on it. Assess if this is due to your partner being not respectful to you. Next comes the friend circle of your kids. Assess if they are in a good friend circle so that they learn good habits based on observations. Also, assess the environment where you live and what kind of learnings it is throwing at your kids.

You can teach your kids about the importance of respect and teach them where they are wrong. In case they carry similar disrespecting behavior with others too, then this is really concerning. You may approach the teachers or someone whom kids respect to coach them on this quality. It is your duty to develop the best qualities in your kids and if it requires some sort of soft punishment, it is considered okay from a parenting perspective. In spirituality, it is the primary responsibility of the parents to develop the child till s/he becomes independent. You also need to assess your own behavior and find methods that kids can learn and appreciate.

16. Is it ok to have sexual relationship with more than 1 partner? What does Gita say about such things?

When sexual activities are undertaken only for sensual pleasure, it is considered animalistic. So sexual relationship with anyone other than your spouse is considered Adharma (against dharma). This is not right. This indicates your immaturity to differentiate between right and wrong. This shows your lust. You are cheating on yourself. And with such behavior you should not expect trust from others. Gita teaches us to stay away from sensual (body) pleasures as far as possible.

17. I am not able to afford a costly lifestyle for my family. However, my family expects it from me. What should I do?

There is no end to expectations in life. You must raise your family, and give them the right knowledge, food, and security to the best of your abilities. It seems you are giving them everything except the right knowledge. Or there is a possibility that your family is under the false impression that you can afford more than what you have. Be honest with your family. Tell them the truth about your financial situation.

It seems you have not understood the real needs of life. The materialistic things which we relate to lifestyles and show-off should never be the focal point of life. There is no end to lifestyle. Don't run after a lifestyle. This will break you and your family. You need some coaching on life, the right things in life, and how to manage the relationship. Consult some life coach.

18. I am not able to put values into my kids. What should I do to improve them?

Don't blame yourself for everything. First, assess what you have done so far to teach values to your kids and understand where you have gone wrong. It could be the methods you used to teach your kids which are not working or it could be because of other factors which you have not considered. You may take the help of an external teacher who can bring those values to your kids as one of the methods. You need to be very clear on what values you really value and what is that you are expecting from kids. Also, assess if are there any problems with your expectations? It is parents' duty to imbibe good values in kids. So, it should be your duty and not an expectation.

Assess your behavior, the behavior of your spouse, and the environment in which your kids are growing. Be honest to assess if there are problems in any of those. Many times, we assume, we are perfect and there are expectations from everyone around us including kids. The same applies to others too. Others also expect some behavior from us. And when there are gaps, the behavior of people differs. These are natural. This is how our mind works. We perceive things differently. And this difference is not bad. There are ways to address problems and differences. However, the problems must be very clear. You must split your problem into multiple categories and assess what is wrong, and where! Kids have a learning mind and they can be taught values over time. The same applies to us too as an adult or mature individual.

19. How do make a balance in the family?

Good behavior is a reflection of balance within a family. The behavior of everyone in the family should be authentic and not fake. It should reflect the intellectual maturity of everyone within the family. When we view others with respect and care from a spiritual lens, our perspective changes on people. Having said this, everyone is responsible for the balance in the family. When it comes to you, you must apply a spiritual lens for maintaining a balance in the family. That implies you need purity of mind, control of senses, sacrifice, simplicity, non-violent, peace, and modesty. You are responsible for your actions not for others, so you can do your bit better. But you should be situation neutral even if something is not balanced within the family. You can teach good qualities and behavior to others too.

Broadly if there is the existence of respect, care, integrity/honesty, sacrifice, control, and no expectations from others within a family, it can live a balanced life.

20. Shall I pick spirituality over family life?

Spirituality does not ask you to give up your family. Both can happen hand in hand. You have a set of duties for your family which you must fulfill. At the same time, you have duties towards your purification (self-improvement) which is nothing but spirituality. Spirituality is aimed at gaining the ultimate peace. It does not ask you to compromise. It asks you to give up your bad qualities and demands the sacrifice of anger, lust, greed, attachments, and desires. If you view everything from an angle of duties, you will be able to do justice to both your family and yourself.

MANAGING EMOTIONS

21. How to manage the negative emotions?

Negative emotions are developed based on our poor experiences in this world. Many times, it is triggered due to our disappointments, anger, greed, and fear. One must realize the trigger point that is invoking negative emotions. Once we can identify the triggering points (e.g., a situation that creates discomfort or fear in the mind), we can manage it better.

The problem with many of us is that we do not what is causing the emotional hijack. Even when you are aware of it, you lack the methods to train your mind on how to absorb those emotions. Such negative signals must be neutralized immediately otherwise it hijacks our brain. There are various methods available today that can control emotions such as meditation, eating a good diet, exercising, walking, listening to music, reading books, etc. Assess what gives you a boost or a positive sense of feeling amongst them. That could work as a neutralizer for the negative impulses when they hit your brain. You are trying to nullify the impact of these impulses with diversion of mind. It has to happen immediately, otherwise, you will get hijacked by your brain. Train, your mind with a positive attitude towards life. You can also lean toward spirituality if you are a believer in God. Find a good teacher who can guide you here. Negative emotions can be easily managed. It needs self-management first. Make your mind your friend first for handling negative emotions. Negative emotions work like a bad signal to the brain but the brain treats them as a life-threatening signal. Not all negative emotions are life-threatening, so why deal with all negative emotions in the same way? Handle them with a change in your perspective towards life. With this method, things will automatically improve for you.

22. Is spirituality the only answer to managing negative emotions?

There are many methods available to manage negative emotions. Negative emotion trigger requires immediate distraction of mind to avoid the trap of emotional (amygdala) hijack within our brain. You can either pick things that give your relief or slows down your brain activities. This could be as simple as watching your favorite channel on TV or listening to music, meditating, swimming, or even eating something that gives pleasure. You may pick up the phone and talk to your friends or family members for distracting your mind. And it works. The other methods include nature's watch, meditation, playing with kids, and reading books. If the negative emotions are beyond control, then there are methods to slow down the brain medically. In that case, you may consult a doctor who will help with controlling the negative hormones that are getting generated in your brain when you are under influence of emotions.

23. Between Spirituality and Medical methods, which is the right way to handle emotions?

Spirituality is self-interest based. You cannot force spirituality on people. A person suffering from the severe impact of negative emotions, may not be able to focus even if s/he selects meditation for calming down. Without trust and belief, no one will ever pick a spiritual path. It is a natural progression of individuals. Spirituality helps with emotional management as a systematic process. On other hand, medical science is useful when a person is not able to manage emotions by themself or even with the help of a guru or a teacher. It requires the intervention of others (doctors) to cure you when the meditation process is not helping. Both methods are good. If you can self-manage your emotions, you do not need a doctor. If you struggle to control your emotions or are in a poor state of mind, you must consult the doctor immediately. Everyone is suffering from emotional management in today's society, so, therefore, seeking help is the best option. The good news is it is curable so relax and enjoy life.

24. Why do we fail to manage our emotions despite knowing they harm us?

Our brain is a complicated machine. You may also call it a chemical factory of hormones. Many hormones get secreted within our brain. Based on how we have trained our brain to handle situations and our memory, our brain behaves differently. It produces different hormones (various stress hormones or happy hormones) automatically.

You have no control over the secretion or production of these hormones. Not all hormones are harmful. When you experience love, care, and respect, the happy hormones are produced in your brain and you feel good. When we are not feeling good (due to anger, frustration, fear, loss, hate, etc), the brain secretes the stress hormones, that make us dull, pathetic, and stressed. Excessive and repetitive secretion of the stress hormones makes us vulnerable to the situation and stops our brain's activity to behave normally.

We fail to manage emotions primarily because of our bad experiences that are stored in our memory. They are deep-rooted within our long-term memory. We must let go of some of the negative experiences. That is the best way to get rid of the negativity of the brain. This is cleansing of the brain. We must learn to calm our brain and feed it with positive signals or experiences. Erase your past poor experiences and refresh them with new memories so that our brains can work in our favor. Please remember that your brain is your greatest friend as well as the worst enemy too. So be careful with your enemy. The more you greet your enemy (negative emotions), the more harm it will cause you.

25. Who is responsible for emotional weakness in a person? Is it the surrounding, family, society, or the person itself?

The person is responsible here. The primary reason is emotional control is our responsibility. We are responsible for self-care and self-control. Emotions are our property as it gets generated or developed within our brain. We produce it, so we own it. It is your brain so you are the owner of it. Therefore, you should take credit as well as blame for your emotions.

When we fail here, that implies the outsiders are controlling us, controlling our emotions, our feelings, our anger, etc. When you become out of self-control, you are bound to harm yourself. Emotions are generated within our brain and we should never give control of our brain to others or their actions. There will be situations in life, where people will irritate you, annoy you, cause anger, fear, and even threaten you. It is your ability to manage those signals in your brain so that you balance them.

26. Are emotions good or bad for humans?

Emotions are good as well as bad in nature. There are positive emotions and negative emotions that get triggered in our brain. The positive emotions give a feel-good feeling (due to love, respect, care, win, success, etc) whereas negative emotions make us a victim of stress. Negative emotions tigress stress which leads to anger, frustration, and anxieties. The chronic anxieties if not treated properly become depression. We should learn to understand our emotions, and how our brain behaves when we are emotional. The awareness itself can help to reduce the impact of negative emotions on us dramatically.

27. What is the triggering point of our negative emotions?

Triggers for negative emotions can be different. Many times, it is due to failure to match the expectations (our expectations and that of others from us). The unfortunate events in life (breakup, loss of family member, divorce, abuse, cheating, etc) also trigger negative emotions. A few times, when you feel you are not perfect (or doubt your capabilities), it also leads to negative emotions. Our parameters of success, when not met lead to negative emotions. Failures in life and fear are the major reasons for people getting a victim of negative emotions. In short, when you are not able to calm down your mind or balance the impulses that clutter your mind, you get negatively impacted by emotions.

28. Why do people fail to realize that negative emotions are hurting them?

Our brain is a complex machine. It decides one thing at a time. And any decision of the brain is based on thousands of signals (impulses, sense responses, memories, etc) that are processed in nanoseconds or even faster by the decision-making authority of the brain (frontal lobe). When we are impacted by negative emotions, our brain (amygdala) takes over the charge and operates in SOS mode (i.e., it appeals for urgent help to other parts of the brain). SOS stands for "Save our Ship". The response to such an aspect is either fight or flight or freeze with all energy that we have. This is how we are programmed by God. We cannot make any logical or useful decision when we are under the influence of negative emotions. The brain reads everything as a threat signal to life. Our brain gets busy producing multiple stress hormones during that time to alert the body parts to take actions related to fight, flight, or freeze. In short, our brain ignores everything else as a priority during that time till it gets the feedback signals back from our body. The body sends back one of the brain signals related to "threat averted" or "still under threat" as per our reactions. This is what happens inside the body and brain in those fractions of seconds.

When we are under the influence of negative emotions, we do not accept any advice, everything looks suspicious or doubtful to us, and we do not trust anyone including ourselves. The reason for it is due to the brain is operating in SOS mode and wants to save us first before anything else. The problem with many of us is that we fail to classify negative emotions into "severe" "manageable" or "somewhat manageable" categories. Over years we have programmed our brain in a wrong way to even treat the "manageable negative signals" as "severe life-threatening signals". And our perception of life has gone negative when we are under the attack of negative emotions. This needs a change in perspective. It is curable. It is normal. We all face it in different proportions. Some can realize it early, some realize it late and for a few, it needs intervention by a doctor or a spiritual guru to get a cure.

29. What can we do to protect ourselves from an emotional breakdown?

You need to take life a bit easy. Don't make your brain operate in emergency mode always. The brain is like a machine that also needs rest and regular maintenance. We must feed good food (thoughts) to our brain regularly, change our life patterns, identify what is causing the emotional hijack, and list it down. There are methods to retrain your brain so that your negative perception gets cleared over time. Mediation can help, spirituality can help, and Sleep can help. Music can help, Walk and swimming can help. Many things are of our liking category that you need to feed your brain to slow down your noisy mind. If we are still not able to calm it down and feel we are not improving, you can consult doctors. There are proven treatments available to cure you. There is no need to panic as we all face emotional breakdowns at different stages of life. For a few, their capacity to handle things (emotional hijack) is poor compared to others. This is normal. We are born with different capacities to handle things. We must learn to enjoy life. If we spend our life just worrying about negative things, when will we do other things which we have not yet started? Emotional problems make our minds trouble or stress machines and we lose our cognitive capabilities. We must value this life. If we decide, we can make it beautiful. It is in our hand and not for others to decide how to run and governs our emotions (and indirectly us).

30. How can Bhagavad Gita help in managing emotions?

Bhagavad Gita is all about achieving purity in life. This includes purity of body, thoughts, mind, and actions. This is all about spirituality. It teaches us to identify the right things in life such as Karmayog (doing our duties without any expectations), Gyanyog (learning things to elevate the level of our mind), and Bhaktiyog (to devote our every action to God). This is what it teaches. It teaches us to sacrifice our ego, anger, desire, attachment, and feelings/emotions. It makes us immune to situations. It makes us see God in everyone. It makes us realize that our purpose in life is not to run around for desire, fame, and money but rather to purify ourselves (our negative qualities which include negative emotions) so that we can attain peace. The ultimate peace is also called liberation. Once we start practicing Bhagavad Gita, our brain gets stronger in terms of handling shocks of life. We develop patience and self-control. And once that is built, the emotions do not influence us. We learn to absorb negative emotions. We become a better version of ourselves.

PROFESSION

31. Why there is so much hypocrisy and fake behavior in professional world?

This aspect cannot be generalized. Few good companies are genuine and follow the core values with integrity having good culture. The corporate culture is made up of the people, their behavior, and actions. Leadership plays a critical role in shaping the culture. If leadership at different levels is giving only a lip-service to its culture, the organization becomes a hypocrite in the medium to long term. Such an organization does not succeed in the long run and reaches stagnation very soon.

If the organization becomes a hypocrite, it does not recognize, the performance and values of deserving employees. It is run on the wish or power of individuals rather than on real values and performances. The company becomes ad hoc and autocratic in some sense where processes and policies are not followed uniformly and consistently across the organization. These gaps give rise to company politics and preferential treatment for poor or mediocre performance. And in such an organization, you witness fake behavior across the board.

32. Corporate culture is built on people, their behavior and actions. Can we apply the principles of Bhagavad Gita in the professional world?

Yes, Bhagavad Gita fits in today's corporate environment perfectly. The culture is made up of people first. If there are no people, there will be no actions and behavior. And if the major segment of people or employees are dissatisfied or stressed in the organization, it signals a bad culture. Employee performance and productivity dip when they are not happy and stressed out.

Bhagavad Gita's learnings can help to reduce the stress of employees. Work-related stress is the prime reason for dissatisfaction amongst working professionals these days. This is also termed corporate stress. Bhagavad Gita helps to develop the mind to handle stress and failures through spirituality. Meditation (which mainly helps with focus and relaxation) is one of the techniques that can be practiced within corporate settings. Many companies are conducting stress management techniques for their employees but those are not very effective. Bhagavad Gita teaches how to handle failures, how to learn to become situations agnostics, and how to conduct duties with complete honesty and integrity. All of these can enable to develop the productive workforce. Organizations are hesitant to include spiritual coaching or training as they fear it may be viewed as religious agenda by a few, so in the name of diversity and inclusion, they take shortcuts such as meditation exercises and some other methods which do not work outside the classroom settings.

33. Can a person achieve success in the professional world by following the disciplines or learnings of the Bhagavad Gita?

Bhagavad Gita does not teach to tun after success but rather to chase peace. Success has different meanings in today's world and we often link it to our position, wealth, and financial status. Success cannot guarantee you inner peace, but peace definitely can ensure you feel successful with your actions in life. The teaching of Bhagavad Gita helps to develop confidence and reduces fear. Fear and expectations are the two main things that hinder our mental peace. Gita teaches us to how to get rid of these enemies of life. It helps us to understand how to make a balance in life for a peaceful living. Be it the professional world or the personal, these learnings are essential for us to live an enriching life.

34. The maximum depression is observed amongst the working professionals. What can be done by organizations to overcome it and develop a productive workforce?

The organization must take the stress issues of employees very seriously. Many companies, leave this problem to each employee to figure out and sort on their own. This is unfortunate but the reality of today. Very few responsible companies are focusing on the well-being of employees seriously. The companies need a spiritual and counseling unit that can help employees with their stress and mental health-related issues. This should be run by independent and qualified external professionals (not by HR or cultural teams) who are experts in spiritual and mental health topics.

There should be awareness sessions to make people open up and take raise their issues for advice. The company should also investigate and identify the top reasons for employee stress levels and build a mitigation plan to address it with advice from professionals in this field. If some of these basic steps are followed properly, a company can have much more motivated and productive workforce.

35. Can corporates teach Spirituality? Will, it not creates a religion-based divide?

Spirituality is not about religion. This is a mistake people make. We hardly understand spirituality and carry our assumptions about it. Religions are more about methods and rituals whereas spirituality is about attaining God. This topic is better addressed by professionals in this field. Responsible companies can assess spirituality as a well-being initiative for their staff and engage with experts from respective areas. Corporates cannot teach spirituality but they can facilitate it. Spirituality has nothing to do with religion. It is about attaining inner peace. And anyone who is struggling with it should take it seriously. This is similar to going to doctors and we do not go to doctors as per religion but as per our ailment. There are experts in spirituality who are as good as doctors for mental well-being. We must not find a religious topic in everything to make it controversial and limelight. It is an optional choice. Those who need help can pick it.

36. The professional world is all about competition, money, job titles, power and corporate politics. How can we make ourselves immune from the negatives of the working environment?

We must do our duties with honesty. There should be no compromise in terms of your commitment to work. Corporate settings are mostly based on give-and-take relationships. Employees give their efforts and companies pay them a salary. The dissatisfaction comes in when the efforts to the remuneration equation get imbalanced due to changes in expectations and market conditions.

The negatives in the work environment are driven mostly by the company culture. Employees must assess if the company is becoming the reason affecting their mental health. If so, they must raise their concern with the appropriate authorities. If it is not addressed by the company promptly, the employee can explore other job opportunities in the market. There is little sense in working in a toxic environment that is taking a toll on your mental health and physical health. It is not advisable.

Having said this, due to varied corporate cultures and people behavior, there will be some degree of corporate politics everywhere, and some stress is inevitable. It is up to you if you want to isolate yourself from it or want to be part of it or if you can handle it. The best thing is to isolate yourself or ignore it so that you can focus on your work, your work commitment, and your skills. This is valued by every company. And there will be someone who will notice it. If it does not get noticed, you should change jobs. Spirituality can help to manage the negative emotions that get generated at the workplace due to various reasons. It makes you calm down your mind and handle adverse events with an open mind. It prepares you to be ready for any results and face any situation with more courage and determination. It does not imply; that you make yourself suffer or get suffocated. You always have choices in life. All you need is a balanced and calm mind to assess things holistically and decide what is best.

37. Corporates are firing people randomly. What can corporates learn from Bhagavad Gita?

Corporates operate primarily on profits and numbers. They need a balance between finances and people. The biggest assets for any company are still people. Innovations are done by people. Tools and technologies are built by people. Technology is applied by people, and businesses us run by people. If a company has zero employees, it is good only on paper. When companies take shortcuts or drastic measures related to people's scrutiny, it has an impact on them in the short to medium terms. It impacts its brand; it loses top talent and faces challenges in hiring and retention. To address this and to keep the rhythm or momentum, companies adopt various shortcuts which harm them in the medium to long term. Net-net does not offer any kind of competitive advantage to companies when they fire people. It gives them some more life/time in case it is the risk of closing (classical examples are start-ups) in terms of some financial cushion due to cost savings. But this is how corporates are designed to operate. Very few responsible companies take a holistic view when it comes to firing employees. This should be managed professionally so that it does not affect employees mentally, emotionally, and harshly. Corporates can learn various things from Bhagavad Gita ranging from respect for the individual to humility, parity to social responsibility. It can learn diversity and inclusion, integrity, professionalism, and decisiveness.

Corporates are essentially nothing but people. The board members to CXO to Janitor all are people with different virtues and values. Bhagavad

Gita is primarily for the people (including corporates employees) and it helps to develop strengths to face any adversaries in life (including firing cases or much more severe situations in life). It helps for mental strengthening, teaches giving up our greed and expectations, and manage the impact of negativity and negative situations on our life. It teaches sacrifice that brings purity of mind and soul. There are hundreds of things to learn from the Bhagavad Gita or other similar scriptures. All are teaching you to be a good human being.

38. What are the biggest mistakes many professionals are doing today when it comes to money, accumulations, lifestyles, etc?

The biggest problem with many working professionals is they do not know "what is enough" for them and "what will make them satisfied". Every professional is running after either money, power, role, job title, status, or visibility in an organization. It is a poor rat race with no end. None of them are learning about the need for mental health and stress management.

More than 90% of working professionals today carry some degree of stress or anxiety. And it impacts their professional and personal life without them realizing it. Unfortunately, this is the reality of today. We are making wrong choices in life. We are running after physical peace (in form of accumulations) instead of mental peace. The bigger problem is many employees do not know how to come out of it or manage mental stress. They hesitate to talk about it, they hardly trust anyone in a corporate setting who is interested in understanding their mental state, they are running like machines that will have a breakdown sooner or later. This needs to stop. We must take help here. Spirituality or medical science can help here. Stress, when becomes unrecognizable, takes the form of acute anxieties which becomes depression in no time. Working professionals must take their mental health seriously as it affects their personal life which has a cascaded impact on work too. This is an infinite loop that either spirituality or a doctor can resolve.

39. What is the right age to retire and move towards spirituality?

The age for retirement is a personal choice. Once you have done your duties towards your family and have some financial cushion to take care of your life, one can think of retirement. Retirement is a step to slow down due to your physical aging and other aspects. If you are physically and mentally fit, you never retire. When your mental health becomes unmanageable, you should take either pause or retire from your work.

Spirituality is not age-based but rather interest-based. People often think that once we get old or get retired, we can think of spirituality. This is unfortunate. Once we start believing that spirituality has a benefit for us, we pick it up. Many times, life circumstances, force us to explore spirituality by force. The Sooner we start spirituality, the better it is for us and our mental health.

40. Which profession is noble as per spirituality?

Any profession that is in serving other humans for a good cause is a noble profession. This may range from medical service, farming, teaching, etc to other sectors too. All professions are noble. The profession that relates to the purification of humans such as the teaching of spiritual knowledge is the most divine. The teacher or gurus who are teaching spirituality are considered the messenger of God as they are teaching peace, purity, love, devotion, and care without any self-interest. Other professions, do not teach these subjects explicitly.

FAME, POSITION AND MONEY

41. Money is everything in today's society. Is there any harm in chasing it?

Money is not bad. The greed for money is bad. We must clear it items of "how much is sufficient" for us. Without such clarity, our desires for wealth will never get fulfilled ever. And we must remember that desires are the reason for our pain, suffering, and anger. We must be careful in terms of what we need from life and where is the end for it. Our life can end at any point in time without any prior notification. If you are able to maintain money and peace, you may continue to chase it. But that would never be the case. Make the right choices in your life. Pick things that matter the most to you.

42. Our society respects us because of our position, fame and our financial position. If across the society that is the norm, why chase spirituality?

We all are running after money, position, fame status, etc. What others are doing does not assure that it is the right thing to do. All the mental health and physical health problems are because of the physical chase we are doing today. None of us are at peace. If that is okay with you, there is no harm in chasing what you are doing. But that is not true. Our mental peace is most important. Today's society is suffering from anger, stress, anxieties, and depression.

Over 90% of working professionals have some kind of work stress which can turn into depression at any point in time if they continue to operate their minds in such conditions. Spirituality helps to attain peace. It helps to improve your focus and gives you the strength to face life with profound knowledge and learning. It is a method to live life better. We must pick what is right for us. We have complete freedom to choose what we think is right for us.

43. The detachment from money is taught in spirituality. Isn't it a foolish thing?

Spirituality does not talk anywhere about detaching from money. It teaches detachment from your desires, anger, lust, anger, attachments, and ego. It teaches you to do your duties for every role that you are playing. Be it as a spouse, father, mother, employee, friend, etc. It does not teach you to be inactive and become a saint or run away to jungles or caves. It teaches us to face life with confidence, faith, determination, and handwork without losing mental balance. It teaches us to make ourselves immune to failures, success, and any outcome in life. Money is needed to run a family, and earning money is part of our duty toward our spouse, kids, and family. So, let's not interpret spirituality without proper understanding.

44. Can we live like a saint or sadhu in this society? Who will feed us if we give up everything?

No one is asking you to become a saint or sadhu. People with a poor understanding of spirituality misread the detachment. There is no need for any changes in your life apart from self-improvement when it comes to spirituality. Feeding yourself is part of your duty or responsibility. You must do the necessary action to deliver that duty. Spirituality teaches us to do our duties with integrity and commitment. Those who want to live like a saint or sadhu can do so. Spirituality does not teach you to become a sadhu. It gives you complete freedom to choose and teaches the repercussions of bad things in your life.

45. If jointing the Ashram or temples is the only objective of life, why to even get there?

None of the principles of Spirituality or Bhagavad Gita ask you to join an ashram or temple. Spirituality can be practiced at home as well without any significant changes to your lifestyle. You need spiritual learnings and practice. All you need is a few good books, time to read and understand, and in a few cases a spiritual teacher who can guide you to clarify your queries and confirm if your approach is correct or not. You must discharge all your duties and responsibilities "as is" without any changes to your lifestyle. However, it needs some time commitment to practice on a regular basis.

46. We see so many greedy saints and conmen around us. None of them are happy. Why to even think of adopting spirituality?

Spirituality is for self-improvement and treating others with respect and care. It does not matter what exists today in this world. This world is not perfect and will never be. Spirituality is for attaining peace. If you are already at peace, you don't need it. Stay happy and follow what you are practicing. If you lack it, you must find ways that can bring your noisy mind at peace. Spirituality is one of the ways to get there.

47. With my money, I can buy peace. And possibly spirituality too. Why should I be bothered about the spiritual Gyan?

Money cannot buy peace. There are hundreds of billionaires dying every year due to mental breakdowns or stress or other reasons linked to their mental health. Spirituality is about self-improvement, self-discipline, and improving your mental capabilities to face the world in any situation. It is a subject of belief.

48. We have to live and face the present time. And the present is a reflection of the society around us. Doesn't it make sense to address our social obligations and excel in them to be happy?

We cannot live happily merely by fulfilling our social obligations. Just recall your last 10 years of life and answer yourself if you were happy all those years? This cannot happen because our life is designed to face the ups and down.

The problems are not with ups and downs in our life but rather with people's inability to cope with the downside of life. We are poor at managing failures, shocks, and surprises in life. This affects our mental capacity over years and we become vulnerable to situations and associated outcomes. We must face the present time without too much impact on us. We must hunt for peace, not momentary pleasure. There is a difference here. Society helps you experience the pleasure of life not the peace of it. Our definition of happiness is materialistic today. Spirituality can teach us to manage our present and future in a dignified way.

49. How spirituality is superior to money, fame and position?

Spiritualty is about union with God. If we assume God is above money, fame and position, then this question is self-explanatory.

50. The reality is that very few followers of spirituality are left in this world. One day spirituality would die, so why waste time on it?

Spirituality is based on individual beliefs. The number of spiritual followers is doubling every year. Every person has some problem in life today that they are struggling to cope with, so practices such as spirituality would continue to expand as people are experiencing its benefits. Inner peace is the biggest challenge across society today. And there is no other method or practice better than spirituality to address it. It is entirely a personal choice. We must get some basics right and do some fact-checking before tagging it as irrelevant or insignificant. This can be practiced and experienced before diving deep into it.

DEPRESSION

51. Depression is not viewed positively in our society. How a person undergoing such things can expect help from family or society?

First thing first, we should not make a big fuss about depression. It is curable both medically as well as spiritually. We all are vulnerable to Depression. So, no need to make it a social taboo. Anyone can get depressed in life at any point in time. So, the more we hide it, the more danger it causes to us.

We must "open up" when we feel depressed. Speak to someone whom you trust about it, your situation, and seek help. The whole world cannot become your enemy (which many people think when they are depressed) all of a sudden. There will be a few who can be relied on. We live in a selfish society so unless you tell people for help, no one will come forward for help on their own with very few exceptions here. There should be no shame in asking for help. After all your situation can lead to the severity or even life-threatening if not addressed properly.

Seeking help from friends, spouses, relatives or doctors could be one easy approach to addressing your depression. The best way is to seek medical help which can give a timely cure for depression. The long-term cure is spirituality which can also be practiced alongside side-lines. The best way is to slow down yourself. The family members must watch if anyone in the family is feeling low for a prolonged time, and assess if their approach or reactions are because of it or if are there any other things that may be making a life of a person miserable who is suffering from depression. Many of us are not able to handle things due to our mental capacity. So, we must be watchful here. Give the necessary support to the person including medical help if needed.

52. Many people struggle to identify the cause of depression or anxieties? How do we identify and deal with it?

When a person is feeling low in energy, not in a mood to engage and isolate themselves from society or from common people for a considerable time (over weeks to months), it indicates the person is suffering from depression or anxieties. Some people become very silent, a few become lose control of their anger and few cry regularly and a few stay fearful all the time. This is the body's reaction to depression. We must identify it early so that it does not become chronic.

You should not give guidance or Gyan to people who are sufferings from depression as their brain is drained/exhausted to accept any advice. Their mental capacity has peaked and they have given up to fight further with their intellect and mind. No advice can help, rather such people need doctors consulting to get some immediate treatment so that their brain activities can slow down. Once the person recovers slightly, he or she can get engaged in other activities which give him or her pleasure or things that can help divert the mind when it senses some negative thoughts or emotions. The person can even try meditation and other activities that help in relaxation. Spirituality is a long-term solution for people who want to come out of depression permanently. We must practice methods to make our brain stronger for different situations, and feeling and learn to control them. We must do spiritual learnings from time to time.

53. Is Meditation or spirituality possible when you are under depression?

No. When someone is under depression, he needs immediate cooling or slowness of mind. Only medical science can offer immediate assistance here. Mediation is helpful when the person is in the initial stages and struggling with stress management. Spirituality takes time and needs practice. A person who is under depression, will not be able to focus and will not appreciate spirituality in the beginning. Once the person realizes that it is the thoughts and emotions that he or she has to manage better, he or can lead to spirituality or other mind management processes. Spirituality is the permanent solution to get rid of depression in long term.

54. What are the main reasons for people getting depressed these days?

It is due to our desires, expectations, fear, and inability to handle failures. In short, you can call it continued or excessive negative experiences from life that lead to depression. We all have some expectations from life, from people around us. When such things do not happen or work in the opposite direction, we feel sad. When such things are repeated over time and we experience such negative elements/activities on us over time, we lose motivation to try things or even give our best. Over time, we get into a state where things do not impress or motivate us as we did not get the adequate or expected output. This makes us full of negativity towards life. The other reasons are related to cheating, abuse, and harassment by others which we are not able to handle.

55. Is the depression curable? What is the best tool to achieve it?

Yes, depression is very much curable. The tools to cure it includes medical assistance, meditation and spirituality.

56. How does spirituality help in Depression?

Depression happens when someone is completely broken from the inside due to repetitive negative incidences that go against the individual's expectations. It is the mental inability to handle the stress and perceiving everything as a threat in life or not relying on anything or anyone around us. The noisy mind in such a time does not want to rest and produces a series of endless negative emotions (and negative hormones in the mind). Spirituality is all about strengthening your mental mind. It makes your mind stronger to absorb the shock of life, the worst that one can think of. It teaches you methods to handle any kind of situation, make yourself immune to thoughts and feelings, its guides you to focus on the right things. In short, it empowers you to live a better life with self-discipline and self-control. It teaches you to handle the worst adversities in life.

57. Society is not appreciative and supportive when it comes to mental health. What is lacking in our society to overcome this challenge?

Our society is lacking basic awareness of depression. And that is the reason it is viewed as a taboo in our society. Mental health is like any other health problem that we face which is curable. Anyone can face it, be it you, me, or any of our family members at any time. It is not a big deal. But this can be life-threatening too. So, it needs attention.

We must learn, what causes depression so that in case we become a victim of it, we are not shocked and have some strengths to face it. The good news is it is completely curable. It needs timely identification and treatment. We must express ourselves from time to time with our close relationship so that someone is watchful of our mental fitness. This is very similar to physical fitness which needs attention from time to time. The only difference is when we are not physically fit, people notice us, and tell us and we also notice ourselves in front of the mirror to check our physical appearance which gives some hints of physical health. However, when we have issues with mental fitness, it is not easily visible to others outside and we may not notice it personally too due to limitations of our mind or lack of our awareness. This is like any health problem that when identified timely, can be treated or handled.

58. Is depression the same as chronic anxieties and fear? How can family members or friends identify it early?

Yes, it is. Chronic refers to anything that continues for a long time. Anxiety or fear that lasts for over weeks to months can become depression. Our mind forms memory and patterns based on repetitive messages (signals) which we send to it. The continuous flow of anxieties signals and fear signals to the mind are stored in it as a pattern and it becomes our memory. The response to stress signals drains our body's energy completely. When this happens, we prefer to stay quiet or isolate ourselves from others or may become violent or angry very quickly. This when becomes repetitive affects our mental health and our ability to fight back with negative emotions. Negative emotions over time caused depression in people.

We must be watchful of the behavior and mood of our dear ones. If you notice continuous changes in the mood of you or your dear ones, this is alarming. Depression is caused by the inability of a person to handle stressful events in their mind. We should talk to people if we notice such changes in behavior. If you find the person dull, non-interested or preferring loneliness over time, then those are early signs of depression. It needs an immediate cure.

59. Who to choose between doctor, psychiatrist and spiritual Guru for treating the Depression?

The first choice should be the doctor. Many times, depression is due to over secretion of hormones. So medically it can be cured. The doctor may advise a psychiatrist based on the assessment of your situation and medical conditions. The spiritual guru can come into the picture once you are medically treated first. The simple reason is spirituality is a long process that needs focus, training of mind, and regular practice. The person who is under depression is not in a position to develop such capabilities in that state of mind where their mind becomes their enemy. Once a person gets some benefits from medical treatment, he or she can explore the spiritual journey to get a permanent solution for depression.

60. Is it okay to talk socially about your depression or mental health with everyone to see help?

Our society is not very open and acceptable to mental health. So, you should talk about it only to the people whom you trust or who can be of some help here. Not everyone is interested in you or your mental health. Unfortunately, that is the reality of our society. We live in a selfish society, so we should be careful whom to talk to and who should be avoided here. However, you should be very open to your spouse, the person whom you trust, and your doctor about your mental health. Hiding mental health can be fatal. Many times, you are the first one to observe yourself first based on your mood swing, interest level, isolation level, curiosity level, behavior, interaction level, socialization level, etc. If you notice, something changing dramatically, you should talk to your family members or spouse about it first. If you are single or have no one to take care of you, you must consult a doctor for help.

DEATH

61. Is death really painful?

Death is the separation of body and soul. When your soul energy is completely drained, the body feels the pain, severe pain too. Many times, fear makes death more painful than death itself. One must accept death and be ready to face it. We should be ready for our death at any time. Yes, this may sound weird but that is the reality of life as death can come at any time without prior notification. Spirituality helps you to face death with ease. It makes you mentally prepared to leave everything, anytime without any guilt including this body.

62. What kind of things do we see when we die?

We often experience what we are attached to just prior to our death. This includes our family, friends, and relatives with whom we have developed love and affection over time. The fear is what we feel the most and the fear of losing things makes us emotionally drained and choked just prior to death. Our brain recalls the flashback of our life and the brain activities are at their peak just before our death. (This is proven medically too on MRI scans of the brain of dying persons)

The other aspects are related to a few people visualizing the image of a ghost (which is also referred to as the God of death) awaiting nearby to carry us away. This is a sort of hallucination of death that makes an individual more terrified. The body becomes slightly cold and the pulse drops down gradually within a few seconds to near zero. Very few people who have been praying and practicing spirituality in their life can imagine God waiting for them for their death. For such people, when they die the pain of death is either zero or minimal. They die peacefully and gracefully. The soul departs from one of the nine openings of the human body (from our 2 eyes, 2 ears, 2 nostrils, 1 mouth, 1 Anus, and 1 Genital). The force of the soul leaving the body is sometimes visible externally on these sense organs after a person has died. Due to fear, few may urinate or pass stool or few may secrete saliva from their mouth or nose at the time of death.

63. Can we make our death a pain-free experience?

Yes. This is possible. Spirituality is the only answer to make death near pain-free.

64. How can we ensure we are not reborn again after our death?

We should pray and surrender to God at the time of our death. This is the only way to ensure, we are not reborn after our death. In Bhagavad Gita, it is stated by Lord Krishna, that when you utter "Om Tat Sat" or any kind of prayer for surrender to God, it will help you for your liberation. Our problems are, not remembering God, at the time of death. This happens because our body is under unbearable pain just before death, the mind is terrified with fear and a common person will never be able to focus on God or recall God at those moments. We need to practice spirituality during our life to recall God at the time of death. Unless it becomes, part of our life routine, we will not be able to recall God. We often recall things, what we store in our memory during our lifetime. If you are storing attachments, fear, and other negative traits, you will recall those during the time of your death. Brains (memory) recall functions work the same way, even just before death. Let's practice spirituality to train our brains for better things in life that give peace. Spirituality is the only solution that helps you with liberation.

65. How can we keep our minds stable during the time of death?

You cannot keep your mind stable just before death if you are not used to controlling your mind. Spirituality is the only way to keep your mind under control and stable both during life and at the time of death. We must practice mind control activities during our life that helps reduce the distraction of the mind. It starts with meditation and ends with surrender to God which we also call as the end state of spirituality.

66. Is it true that everyone who dies, takes a rebirth?

No. Not everyone who dies takes a rebirth. The people who qualify for liberation, are freed from the cycle of birth and death. Our karmic account needs to be carried a zero balance (zero debt) to ensure we are not reborn again. There is the accounting of each of our actions in this life. Our good deeds must overpower the bad deeds. Those who surrender themselves to God at the time of death are the ones who never take any rebirth. For all others, the next life is decided by the karmic account.

67. How our next life is decided after our death?

Our next life is based on the accounting of whether we have elevated our life during this birth or degraded it. We all have a karmic account that decides if we qualify for the next birth or for liberation. If we elevate our life with good deeds (assuming overall karmic balance is positive), we take birth in the higher grades of life i.e., either amongst rich or learned families in our next life. If our karmic balance is negative, we take rebirth in lower grades. In those cases, we may be reborn as animals, insects, or other dangerous creatures whose cognitive capabilities are lower than humans. Those who surrender themselves to God at the time of death, quality for liberation, and such people are not reborn again. The name of God or recall at the time of death nullifies all our karmic balance and makes us free from the cycle of birth and death.

68. What happens after death?

After death, the soul moves out of the body and starts its journey. The soul enters into a new body as per our karma. The other body could be of a human or animal or insect or any other creature. This is decided based on our karmic account. The soul is wrapped within the subtle body which is also called e Manomaya Kosh and Vigyanmaya Kosh). The subtle body is the one that we do not see with naked eyes. This is different than our physical body which dies and is left behind on this earth after our immediate death.

The footprints of our life, and our all actions are stored within the subtle body (the book of our karma, good or bad whatever it may be). The next birth (or yoni) is decided by this karmic book and our soul is on the hunt for a suitable body that matches the karma which we have accumulated till the time of our death. The soul and the body hunting game continues till the soul gets the purifications i.e., the person becomes blissful with purification of all his or her karma. Once the soul is free from all the external sheath or layers, it gets liberation which we also call Mukti or Moksha. The ultimate union of the soul (Atma) with the Param-atma (Almighty) is liberation.

69. Can we make death a pleasing experience?

Not really. We are all fearful and will remain fearful till the last stage of our death. Spirituality helps to minimize the impact of pain and fear related to the separation of the soul and the physical body. Only a very few saints who have developed top expertise in spirituality can feel the pleasure at the time of leaving this world. For others, there will be pain on some level. If we have more attachments and affections in life, the higher the pain at the time of death.

70. Why we are afraid of death?

We are fearful of losing things. This is how we have trained our minds. We are fearful of losing family, accumulations, wealth, relatives, and everything that we love. We have never trained our mind toward death, toward losing everything, and toward spirituality. And when the last minute comes, we are terrified to accept that everything is going to be left behind in a fraction of a second.

The other reason is, the assumption of death that we carry in our mind. We have heard many stories about death. Those remind us of a very painful experience, pain, choking, and unbearable pain. Few talks about, people getting severe punishment just before death. The fear of all those has stayed in our subconscious mind since our childhood. At the time of death, there is a recall of this fear along with the fear of losing everything, everyone. Because of fear we are afraid of death. Fear is the main culprit here. Our beliefs about the death make us afraid of this topic and we avoid talking about it openly.

SPIRITUALITY

71. Is there any God in real? No one has seen God. How can we validate things before starting spirituality?

God is not a material or an object. Neither is a concept. God's presence is well defined in various religious scriptures. It is the superpower that is running and controlling everything. God is a subject of faith and belief. It is a spiritual thing. We as a human, often cannot imagine or visualize things beyond our physical senses. The things which are not visible do not mean it does not exist. It exits but due to our lack of abilities, we cannot see it. The same applies to God. God can be experienced, or even visualized or felt personally. You cannot call people who claim such things insane. Spirituality is all about the experience. It is a subject of belief and faith.

Our science and technology are still not evolved to a level where it can prove the existence of the soul, God, afterlife, etc. There are many subjects that science is still researching for many decades to find some answers to. We even still do not know, how a soul (science calls it Life or heartbeat) enters a fetus within the mother's womb around 6 weeks of pregnancy. We do not know where it disappears immediately after our death. All these aspects have been proven in spirituality thousands of years ago. God is like a super-energy and we are a soul (a small fraction of that energy). The world is not just formed because of the big bang explosions. The world is well organized and carefully created. Explosions do not build or create things with such great perfections. Life has not just happened all of a sudden. We as a human, are not just born as the theory of evolution suggests. None of these can confirm who did the big bang explosion (things do not happen automatability anywhere) and who created the first life. Life cannot happen just as adaptation and accidents.

We all are so perfect and similar in every body organ, cell, nerve, and blood vessel. Look at the tiniest part of your body anatomy and you will witness God's certation within it. We all have a perfect brain, heart, and spinal cord. It cannot happen or get developed automatically, someone has a mega blueprint of it, and there is some architect that has designed it, executing it every day around the world in a similar manner. No need to go anywhere else to find the answer! Have you looked at your brain and heart anatomy? It is so perfectly designed and one of the most complicated engineering that ever existed. It is the same in every human. Who is doing it? Do you think, everything has happened automatically in every human species? No. This makes us believe that there is a superpower who is doing it, running it, and controlling it. You may call it God, Almighty, or any other name. The world and humans are not formed merely because of the big bang and evolution theory.

Also, we must understand that these theories and based on many assumptions. If you are believing those assumptions, you must believe the assumptions of spirituality too. Spirituality is a subject of belief and experiential learning. You can try it, if it works, it is good for you. If it does not work for you, there is no compulsion.

72. How real is the concept of rebirth or incarnation?

The rebirth and incarnations are the subjects of the beliefs. Our science does not believe in it. However, in spirituality, these have been defined and in existence for thousands of years ago.

73. If God is kind to everyone, why there are so many problems in this world?

God has made the world a perfect place at the time of creation. It is the people, their greed, expectations, desires, ego, lust, etc which have created the imbalance in this world. The problems are because of such things not because of God. God is kind to only good people and for others, he is a punisher. He is very just. So, he ensures the dharma (righteous things) in this world.

74. Which God is superior? Which religion does it belongs to?

All Gods are superior. There is only one superpower that is running everything. We may refer to it by different names in a different religion. God does not have a religion. Religions are created by humans to divide people across societies. God has created a division of work based on the qualities of people. For example, people who have good knowledge, are suited for the profession of teaching or sharing knowledge, and people who have servicing mindset can indulge in servicing acts such as a doctor, nurse, Janitor, etc. God has given us the liberty to choose things as per our preferences and likes. We are tied to the religion of our parents at the time of our birth but have the freedom to choose our faith, belief, and profession as per our choices. God has never talked about the division of people but rather about the union. All religions are respectful they represent different people groups and we must respect people. The people are created by the same God, so ultimately, he is our supreme father and we all have some relation to him and amongst ourselves.

75. Does God really have shape or color?

God is the superpower and can exist in both unmanifested as well as manifested forms. Based on the belief system, people pray to any of these forms of God. If someone is praying to the manifested form of God, he or she is free to imagine any shape, color, or size of God. In the end there is only one superpower which is running and governing everything.

76. I have been praying to God since childhood however my pain and sufferings are still the same. Is the God cruel or deaf?

God is neither cruel nor deaf. He plays a passive role in our life. He neither indulges nor participates in our actions. God has given us the freedom to choose our actions and has defined a clear rule book of Karma. God neither take the blame for anyone's karma nor gives credit to anyone for their karma. However, he witnesses each of our karma and makes accounting in terms of our karmic ledger to give us karma phal (report card or fruit of our karma). This report card decides our destiny for the next life. God is everywhere inside us, outside us. So, when we call him with devotion without any desires, he listens to us. You can call him for his blessings and he will come running to you only when you have devoted yourself to him. You offer water, fruit, or leaf as a token of your devotion, he will accept it. He knows everything about us, our past, present, and future. God guides us from time to time and ensures we are on the right path. Our punishments in life are for a reason to change our path toward spirituality and devotion. We need spiritual mastery to understand the signals of God for each of us. Let's not blame God for our pain and sufferings. We are to be blamed for it. It is primarily due to our ignorance. As a human, we tend to take credit for good things and give blame for bad things. We have not even spared god here for our selfish behavior

77. What is the best way to start spirituality?

Spirituality can be started at any point in time in life. Spirituality is often associated with our beliefs and experiences. So, the best phase to start it is during childhood as it helps shape our minds from nascent stages. Spirituality is also related to our past karmic linkages. And that is the reason, that few people are born with spiritual inclination without any reference to spirituality in their family. For many, life experiences invoked or provoke an interest in spirituality. Spirituality can be started with simple meditation, reading spiritual books, or even listening to spiritual knowledge. One may find a guru or teacher who can systematically teach spirituality. Spirituality brings purity to us. It brings purity of mind, thoughts, and actions. Many relate spirituality to religion which is a wrong comparison. Spirituality is for attaining divine peace within. Such ultimate peace comes with faith, devotions, and prayers.

78. Is Bhagavad Gita the only book that teaches spirituality? Is there anything more reliable than Gita?

There are many teaching styles of Spirituality. You may find many books across religions that teach spirituality. Bhagavad Gita is one of the books that help you learn spirituality. Bhagavad Gita is considered the supreme knowledge when it comes to spirituality. This reflects the word of God or song of God which lord Krishna used to teach lessons of life to his student Arjuna. Again, this is a subject or belief, so nothing can be forced or pushed on anyone. People are free to use their intellect to pick and choose any book that gives them peace and lessons of life.

79. Do we need a teacher or Guru to develop expertise in Spirituality? How to identify the one?

We need a guru to learn spirituality. Acquiring new knowledge required a teacher or coach in life. Be it at our school, colleges, or universities or during our working life. We definitely need guidance to learn and master the art of spirituality. For those who are learning spirituality from schooling time, it becomes easy as some foundations are being developed. People who are making a transition to spirituality in midlife, find it more difficult to find a guru or teacher. Their problem is not with the guru but more to assess if the guru is right for them or not. The mind plays the trick here by confusing them and they doubt every person who claims to have spiritual knowledge. Once the spiritual interest is developed, the awareness comes automatically. Bhagavad Geeta says, once you make a step towards the spiritual path, God will help you to achieve it. That implies God will guide you to pick the right guru or will take you to the right guru. We must trust and believe this.

80. How liberation is going to help me? I am more interested in my current life, not in what happens to me after my death.

Liberation is not an award that you will experience in this life. We all are selfish and greedy. Without the understanding of "what's in it for me" greed, we do not get motivated to do things most of the time.

Liberation is not going to help you if you are expecting something in return. Liberation is a spiritual reward that one gets if he or she manages to purify life. If your current life is going well, and you are already at peace that indicates you are already being liberated. You don't need anything. Liberation is the end state. For reaching there you need to learn how to make your current life peaceful, stress-free, attachment-free, ego-free, and desire free. These are the basic things which you need to learn. And these are required for current life. None of us are bothered about what will happen after our death.

We are worried about today, our current life, our current pain and stress, our current challenges, and how to deal with them. We are looking for a method that can teach us such methods which ultimately will take us towards liberation. The journey to a destination should be as important as the destination itself. So, the path to this journey is covered by spirituality and the end destination is the liberation which implies the union with God or ultimate peace. You must make your current life peaceful and no need to worry about death or liberation or after-death experience if it is bothering you more.

DIFFERENT FAITHS AND GODS

81. Why do we follow different faiths?

Our upbringings are different in different families which follow different belief systems. Had it been just one family, we all would be following the same faith. However, that is not the case. Our faiths and beliefs are shaped based on our childhood, family values, our learnings, our environment, our friend circle, and the society around us. Once we believe something to be true, based on our experience, our perception of that subject gets rigid. This is not about right and wrong but more about what we think and believe about it.

Faith and belief are shaped based on our thoughts and our mind's reaction to them. And it does change over time. We have seen people changing their beliefs and faiths as well. People change religion, caste, and change perspectives towards life due to different beliefs and faiths. This is a subject of change and like everything in life, it changes too. And we follow what seems right to us at a specific point in time. Our continuously changing thoughts which we experience personally drives our belief.

82. Can we change our faith and religion?

Our mind is the master to decide our actions. If it convinces us to adapt to a new belief, we accept it. So, people do change their faith and region too. This is not about judging them. This is more about their self-assessment of what is right for them. We must respect it. However, anything that is done with force or with fear is condemnable.

83. Does God have a shape?

God exists in both formless and in form shape. We refer to it as unmanifested and manifested forms of God. If God is the superpower, it is not impossible for him to take any change or form or stay in invisible form. We should not be worried about the shape of God. Our devotion is important to God. Rest all topics are only for debate and for creating unrest in society.

84. Which God is superior, the one with the shape or the one without shape?

Both forms of God represent the same Almighty. It is a pity that people have even divided God in our society based on our beliefs. We must respect each form of God. In the end, there is only one superpower that is running all the universes, every creature, and empowering us. The almighty does not need a shape or form. We need him for his blessings. We can pray to any form of God; in end we are praying to the same superpower which we recall or worship with different names.

85. Why there are so many Gods and goddesses in Hindu religion?

God exists in unmanifested and manifested forms. Based on our beliefs and faiths, we have assumed different forms and shapes of God over time. It is a reflection of our faith. We as a human, mostly relate everything to some shape and form. Our mind recognizes things based on shape and forms. Otherwise, it becomes difficult for us to stay focused and concentrate on things. This has given birth to people's creativity, imagination, and experiences. The different forms of God reflect the same across religions. It reflects our faith and belief. We must respect every form of God be it formless or with different forms.

86. If God is one, why do people pray to different gods in a different religion?

We often do things that we find or perceive as right. We follow different belief systems in our society. This is based on our upbringing, environment, and society. The payers, their forms, God, and their forms are different in a different religion. We have been taught different religious learnings since our childhood by our parents, and teachers and that becomes our belief largely. Since there is a difference in the methods used in each family, we pick up similar things for prayers. The different types of prayers and Gods are due to differences in our society. The good news is we all believe in the same superpower and we assume there is just one superpower. We may call it or refer to it with different names.

87. Is it necessary to sacrifice food and water and conduct a fast for prayers? What does Bhagavad Gita say about such things?

God does not need anything from us. He is the superpower and has everything. So, the prayers, and sacrifice reflects our respect for him. The sacrifice has different meanings in different religions due to the various belief systems. We must respect it. As per Bhagavad Gita, we should sacrifice our negative qualities. This includes the sacrifice of ego, anger, attachments, desires, lust, etc. These create bondage in this world and are the main reasons for our pain and suffering in this world. As a human, irrespective of our belief system, we all admit that these are not good things for humans. So, we must make some attempts to get rid of these bad qualities in ourselves.

88. Why the world is so disorganized, everyone is suffering. Can't God fix it for all?

The world is disorganized not because of God but because of people. God created a beautiful world at the time of the formation of this earth. Over time, people have changed. People have moved from a Satvik nature (pure form) to tamasic and rajasic nature (both tamasic and rajasic represent impurities in us). Because we developing self-centred qualities, we have ruined this world. It is our ego, attachment, lust, greed, and desires that have to change our original form and purity. We have to fix ourselves first. Let's not blame God for everything and rush to him for our every problem.

Unless we purify ourselves again, the world will become more and more pathetic and dangerous to live in. God has a final solution to these problems too. He gives us chance to improve repeatedly so that we live peacefully and allow others to live peacefully. And in end, he destroys the world and recreates it. God can fix everything.

89. God is very powerful and punishes people. Do we pray to him because of fear?

The majority of us pray to God because we need something from him in some form. Be it wealth, good relationship, a loving family, status in life, better lifestyle, peace of mind, etc. These are our materialist expectations from God. We all have it, so if we have some trust or belief in God, we ask for things that we lack. And we have been taught that God is very kind and if we pray to him, he offers blessings. This is one of the main reasons why we pray to God.

The other category of people includes those who believe that God punishes our bad deeds and poor actions, so they do not want to get punished. To keep their punishment level to low, such people offer prayers so that God can forgive their mistakes. This type of prayer is driven by fear. Again, this is based on the belief that God is very kind. The third category of people is the one, who wants to get rid of their impurities of life and past life and seek permanent union with God. Such people are spiritual. In summary, it is our greed, fear, expectations, and devotion that make us pray to God.

90. What is the best way to please God as per Bhagavad Gita?

God does not need anything from us. So, we cannot please him with our actions. He is not like people who get pleased with something. However, God loves and cares for people who possess divine qualities. Such people have committed their lives to the care of others without any self-interest. Such people are pure souls and are representative of God in this world. God loves purity of soul and such devotees. Any of us who decides to purify ourselves and make some effort here will definitely get the attention and love of God. We need to start our spiritual journey. This is what is clearly written in Bhagavad Gita once a person starts a step toward God (spirituality), God will ensure that he is being taken care of by him. Spirituality is a purity process that ultimately helps us unite with God. Many of us call it liberation or Mukti.

SOUL

91. Is the soul real? Medically or scientifically, it is not proven. Why should we believe in it?

Our body runs on some energy. This energy in spirituality is referred to as soul whereas in medical science it is referred to as heartbeat. So, the energy is real which gives all of us life. There are many things that are not yet proven by science and technology including soul energy. No doctor or scientist can tell you from where the heartbeat enters a fetus (a baby inside a mother's womb within 6 weeks of gestation) but even they believe in it. We have ECG machines where you monitor the heartbeats in form of signals. One must ask, himself or herself where this signal goes once someone dies. If you assume that it gets dissolved in the environment then, you can call the environment God. God is everywhere. In spirituality, the soul is a portion of God's energy. Our beliefs are not always based on facts. Believes are the subject of experience and not a subject of evidence or proof. Spirituality is a subject of belief whereas science is a subject of evidence. So, they will never align.

92. If the soul is pure and part of God, why does it gets punished for the next life?

Soul once gets liberated (pure), it gets dissolved in God. It is part of God; however, God does not accept anything that is impure or incomplete. Our soul (when inside our body) is influenced by mother earth (Prakriti) and works under the influence of Prakriti's three qualities i.e., Stava Guna, Rajo Guna, and Tamo Guna. Based on our intellect, we can handle the influence of these gunas on us (and indirectly on the soul). Our body gets impure due to our poor actions. And the soul is being held responsible for it.

Every experience of life and its footprints are stored in our memory. This is not just the physical memory (within our Brain) but also in the subtle body that our eyes cannot see. The subtle body includes layers of Manomaya Kosh and Vigyanmaya Kosh. Our intellect is stored in Vigyanmaya Kosh whereas our emotions are stored in our Manomaya Kosh which includes our fear, anger, greed, happiness, etc. When we die, our physical body gets destroyed however our subtle body remains. This subtle body covers the soul and cannot be burnt or buried. Since the subtle body is impure due to our pending desires, greed, lust, etc, the soul does not get liberated freely.

Our soul is wrapped by our subtle body. If our karmas are not good, that implies our soul is not pure due to the impurities around it in the forms of Manomaya and Vigyanmaya Kosh (of the subtle body). The next life is decided by the overall karmic account that is based on the overall purity of Manomaya and Vigyanmaya Kosh. The soul is god's energy (which is already pure), Its job is to guide us or empower us (the body) during our life so that our body does not get indulge in poor deeds. But when the soul, enters a human body, it forgets its original purpose due to the influence of Prakriti (Maya) which is more powerful than the soul. We perform an action based on our body; the soul does not do anything. It just witnesses things when inside a body. The punishment is given to the body (and to the soul too) which resides in the body. This indirectly is a punishment to the soul as failed to purify the body as a teacher and a guide. And so, it does not get liberated after our death if we have impurities. And is also remains trapped for various cycles in different body types.

93. Why the soul needs a body and why does it leave a body?

Our body runs on energy. We call it soul energy. Energy needs a medium (e.g., body) to express and act. We do our karma with our body and our body is run by energy. Soul and body represent our existence in this world. Both need each other for manifestation. God has given its portion of energy to us in form of soul energy. Soul energy is pure divine energy, it does not need anything from us. The soul empowers the body to do karma. It gives energy to the entire body so that it can function properly.

When we are born inside a mother's womb, there is a fetus without any energy (heartbeat) inside it till 6 weeks of gestation. When parents desire a child and start expectations or dreams for the fetus, God sends its energy (appropriate soul) inside the fetus to give the fetus life. This is how a soul enters a body. Without a soul, we are like a dead body. The same applies to a fetus inside a mother's womb, it is dead without any energy. The soul is needed to empower the body. We have seen many fetuses terminating without taking birth. This is because they do not get the blessing of god's energy.

The journey of the soul is decided by the Almighty. The soul empowers the body so that body can function in its entirety to do karma or actions. When the body deteriorates due to aging or illness, it fails to perform the required action on the soul energy. This is similar to a light bulb that gets electric energy to illuminate light in a room. When the bulb gets fused or damaged, the room needs a new replacement bulb. Along similar lines, when our body is not fit for action, that condition is similar to a damaged bulb that needs replacement so that energy can be utilized properly. You may also relate it to changing torn clothes and wearing a new one. Soul also hunts for a fit body to function and perform actions that are pending or due for it to accomplish (God decides if the soul qualifies for liberation or needs a transfer to a new body to perform the pending karma). The soul is pure and it empowers us to perform our best karma to our full potential (via body) when inside a fit body. if something (body) is unfit, it is of no or little use and gets destroyed, the same applies to our body.

94. How can we convince ourselves that we are not a body but a soul?

With your power of the mind, we can convince ourselves of anything. Spirituality helps us to reinforce that belief. We can easily convince ourselves that our body is temporary. We have witnessed so many deaths in this world already so we know for sure that the body has a temporary existence. The soul is life energy and this is also something known to everyone. So rather than struggling to assess whether are you a body or a soul, you think of yourself as a whole that contains both body and a soul. You must do your meaningful karma that matters the most. Soul existence cannot be proven or measured or seen so there is no point in finding a difference. Just enjoy your life. But your karma should be good without causing harm and danger to others. Do good deeds that matter the most.

95. How the soul decides if it needs to move upwards (higher abode) or the lower abode?

The soul does not decide its journey on its own. This is guided by the Almighty. When our karmic account is positive i.e., we have done more good deeds than bad ones, we qualify for higher abodes as per Bhagavad Gita. If our karmic account is purest, we get the liberation i.e., we get a place in Vishnuloka and our soul dissolves within the Almighty. When our karmic account is negative, our soul is sent to the lower abodes and we are forced for rebirth and to find a suitable body of lower grade species such as animals, inspects, etc that matches our karmic value. Let's not worry too much about what abode we will go to after death. We should make this life meaningful and peaceful, there is no point in worrying about the next life or subsequent lives thereafter.

96. At what point in time, the soul is assessed for the next birth or liberation?

The next life for the soul is decided at the time of death. God knows our past, present, and future. And based on the last breath that we exhale and based on our mental state (thoughts) at that point in time, our soul's next journey is decided. The soul's purity at the time of death decides if it will move to a higher Abode (e.g., Heaven) or a lower one (e.g., hell). The detailed journey of a soul after birth is covered in detail in "Garuda Purana" which covers the conversation between lord Vishnu and Garuda (Eagle) related to the journey of the soul. The soul does not get the next body immediately and it has to go through the pain or reward based on the karmic account balance before getting a new body or before getting liberated. Few souls that experience accidents, suicide, and killing face the maximum wait till they get a new body. There is different belief in different religion related to rebirth, and reincarnation. None of these aspects can be proven. We must accept whatever makes sense to our minds.

97. Soul is considered as energy. If so, why can't we capture it like other energies?

Science is not able to capture, assess and analyze every type of energy. There are still many energy types that we have not yet discovered in this world. There were many experiments that were done in the past on dead people to understand how the body, mind, and heart react at the time of death and various signals were monitored. Research is still going on in different parts of the world to capture the soul's energy or at least navigate its path or measure it with some instruments or waves. None of it has been successful. It is unlikely that as a human we would be able to resolve or capture the mysteries of the soul ever using physics, science, or technology. This is like making failed attempts to capture God or its soul energy to claim superiority over anything.

98. How does the soul remember our past karma?

When we are born, we are born with some portion of our past memories. This is evident because few people are born gifted with amazing powers and unique capabilities. Like any newborn, majority of us learn based on observations, learnings, and experience. So, something that comes as an inborn talent is gifted by God. The soul energy when it moves from one body to another moves along with a layer of the subtle body (which is the non-physical body). This contains our past Karma i.e., our past memories, pending desires, lust, anger, etc. When the soul transition to a new body, this whole bundle gets into the womb of a mother. Once a newborn develops, his brain gets empowered with those memories or past karmic residues. So, we must remember that some of the past karmic records have some influence on us. Few people are very fearful since the time of birth, few are terrified of water, and heights, few are disappointed in life since birth, and all are due to the past karmic influence on this life. So, if you think you are not born lucky, there is a high possibility of it. It does happen. But we should not blame the past for everything, and start living in the reality of the present and do our actions to purity ourselves in the new life.

99. If the soul moves to a new body immediately after our death, how come it decides which body to pick up and where?

The soul does not move to a new body immediately. It may take up to 30 days if the karmas of a person are good and if s/he had died a natural death. Any all cases, there is an accounting that decides or next life and the body that qualifies to carry our soul. The time frame could vary up to a year tour for the poor soul for the earth to different abodes that got punished for bad karma for the body. The next life could be in form of a human, insect, animal, or any other creature.

Accidental deaths, suicide, and killings are the worst categories of death where the soul struggle to move out of the earth. Such souls get trapped for a much longer time and may run around as a ghost and face hardship but such energies are not visible. No one can see any soul. Our eyes are not capable of it. In a few of such accidents or suicide cases, the soul may not ever get liberated from the earth. We must use this life meaningfully. Let's make our life and death a meaningful experience. We must learn to prepare for our death or at least be ready for it. This is the hard reality and the more we run away from it, the more fear we have for life and death.

100. Can two souls recognize each other and talk to each other?

Yes. As per "Garuda Puran", a soul can recognize its relatives, and families as well as the people who have passed away from this world after their death. Soul-to-soul communication is possible as per spiritual belief. Again, this is a belief that no one can prove as right or wrong.

About The Author

Girish Joshi is a technology executive with over 24 years of experience while working with leading global technology companies. Having worked across 15 different countries in various leadership roles, he has observed company cultures, corporate dynamics, and people behavior at different levels very closely. Girish Joshi has been identified as "Top 10 Chief Digital Officers in India 2021" by the CEO Insights magazine. He has achieved top academic records during his schooling, Engineering, and MBA times.

He has been very successful professionally and personally during his life. Girish is a strong believer in living a principle-driven life. He has observed stress and depression as common problems across communities globally. This book is an attempt to help people who are not able to cope with stress and missing inner peace in their life due to a variety of reasons.

The book first explains why our mind does not recognize the danger of stress, and depression and fail to overcome it. It explains the reasons for our pain and suffering and how we can leverage spirituality and our intellect to overcome stress for attaining inner peace. The book is based on the learnings from Bhagavad Gita, Anatomy study of the human brain, and various analysis related to various problems of our life.